Y0-DWK-986

Contents

Appendixes

TECHNOLOGY
FOR RESULTS

•••

Developing Service-Based Plans

DIANE MAYO
for the
PUBLIC LIBRARY ASSOCIATION

AMERICAN LIBRARY ASSOCIATION

Chicago   2005

While extensive effort has gone into ensuring the reliability of information appearing in this book, the publisher makes no warranty, express or implied, on the accuracy or reliability of the information, and does not assume and hereby disclaims any liability to any person for any loss or damage caused by errors or omissions in this publication.

Composition by ALA Editions in Stempel Schneidler and Univers using QuarkXPress 5.0.

Printed on 50-pound white offset, a pH-neutral stock, and bound in 10-point coated cover stock by McNaughton & Gunn.

The paper used in this publication meets the minimum requirements of American National Standard for Information Sciences—Permanence of Paper for Printed Library Materials, ANSI Z39.48-1992. ∞

Library of Congress Cataloging-in-Publication Data

Mayo, Diane, 1950–
    Technology for results : developing service-based plans / Diane Mayo for the Public Library Association.
        p.   cm. — (PLA results series)
    Includes bibliographical references and index.
    ISBN 0-8389-3550-8
    1. Public libraries—Information technology—United States—Planning—Handbooks, manuals, etc. 2. Public libraries—United States—Automation—Planning—Handbooks, manuals, etc. 3. Library planning—United States—Handbooks, manuals, etc. I. Public Library Association. II. Title. III. Series.

    Z678.9.A4   U654 2005
    025.1'974—dc22   2005003334

Printed in the United States of America

09   08   07   06   05   5   4   3   2   1

Figures

Acknowledgments

The author would like to thank Sandra Nelson, senior editor, and June Garcia, associate editor, of the Results Series for their invaluable help in writing this book. Their deep knowledge of the challenges facing public libraries and their insightful questions about the processes of technology planning pushed me to far better work than I could have done on my own. I also want to thank my husband, James K. Barrentine, whose knowledge and advice are incorporated throughout this book. Finally, thank you to Greta Southard, executive director of the PLA, who continues to believe in and provide support for the Results Series.

Introduction

Managing a public library has always been hard work, and it is becoming even more difficult under the twin pressures of restricted public funding and rapid change. The Public Library Association (PLA) plays a major role in providing the tools and training required to "enhance the development and effectiveness of public librarians and public library services."[1] Since 1998, PLA has provided support for the development of a family of management publications that are being used by library administrators, staff, and boards around the country to manage the libraries in their communities more effectively. The five publications available in 2005 are

> *The New Planning for Results: A Streamlined Approach*[2]
>
> *Managing for Results: Effective Resource Allocation for Public Libraries*[3]
>
> *Staffing for Results: A Guide to Working Smarter*[4]
>
> *Creating Policies for Results: From Chaos to Clarity*[5]
>
> *Technology for Results: Developing Service-Based Plans*

In 2004, PLA executive director Greta Southard and the members of the PLA board made a long-term commitment to the Results Series. Sandra Nelson was selected to be senior editor of the series and June Garcia was asked to serve as associate editor. The PLA board authorized the funding required to publish five Results books between January 2005 and July 2007—approximately one every six months. PLA issued a Request for Qualifications to people who were interested in writing for the series and received responses from ten, four of whom were selected. This publication, *Technology for Results*, is the first of the four new publications. It will be followed by *Demonstrating Results: Measuring the Impact of Library Services on Users*; *Managing Facilities for Results*; *and HR for Results: The Right Person for the Right Job*.

All of the Results Series publications—both current and proposed—provide a fully integrated approach to planning and resource allocation, an approach that is focused on creating change—on *results*. The underlying assumptions in each of the books are the same:

> Excellence must be defined locally. It is a result of providing library services that match community needs, interests, and priorities.
>
> Excellence does not require unlimited resources. It occurs when available resources are allocated in ways that support library priorities.

Excellence is a moving target. The best decision-making model is "estimate, implement, check, and adjust"—and then "implement, check, and adjust again."

The Results Publications

The foundation of the Results Series is *The New Planning for Results: A Streamlined Approach. The New Planning for Results* describes a library planning process that is focused on creating an actual blueprint for change rather than a beautifully printed plan for your office shelf. As shown in the Planning for Results model (figure 1), the process starts by looking at the community the library serves in order to identify what needs to happen to improve the quality of life for all of the community's residents. Once the community's needs have been established, library planners look for ways the library can collaborate with other government services and nonprofit agencies to help meet those needs. This, in turn, provides the information required to establish the library's service priorities.

FIGURE 1
Planning for Results Model

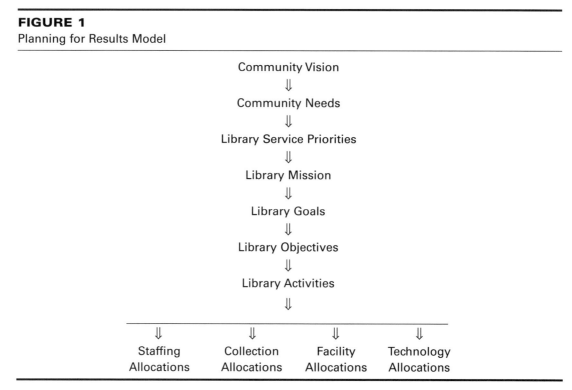

Source: Sandra Nelson and June Garcia, *Creating Policies for Results: From Chaos to Clarity* (Chicago: American Library Association, 2003), xii.

The planning process includes significant participation by community residents who represent all of the constituencies served by the library: parents and children, working adults and seniors, businesspeople and civic leaders, students and educators, the various racial, ethnic, and religious groups in your community, government and nonprofit leaders, and all of the other groups that together create your unique community. By involving all of these groups in your planning process, you ensure that the services you provide are really what community residents want—and not what you or your staff or board think (or wish) that they would want.

Because *The New Planning for Results* is focused on identifying and implementing the activities that will help library managers and staff to accomplish community-based goals and objectives, the decisions that are made are sure to affect every part of the library's operations. Every library manager, library staff member, and library board member is going to have to become used to the idea of continuously evaluating all of the services and programs the library currently provides and all of the technologies that support those services in the context of the library's identified priorities—and then be willing to make any changes that are necessary. Changes don't happen because we want them to or hope they will. Changes only happen when we do things differently—and that means finding new resources or reallocating the resources we have.

Over the past ten years, the rapid changes in the technologies that library staff use to deliver services and support their administrative functions have made managing technology resources particularly challenging for library boards and managers. The second book in the Results Series, *Wired for the Future: Developing Your Library's Technology Plan*, was published in 1999.[6] It was designed to help library managers develop a comprehensive technology plan that would provide a blueprint for creating or expanding the library's basic technological infrastructure.

Today virtually every public library has an established technological infrastructure. However, library managers are still grappling with the problem of managing that infrastructure. It seems as if there is a new cutting-edge technology every week. Some staff want to have the newest and most innovative technologies. Other staff would prefer that the doomsday scenarios about Y2K had come to pass. In this new environment, the information in *Wired for the Future* was not as useful as it had been when those earlier technology decisions were being made. The question is no longer "What should our basic infrastructure include?" The questions now are "What technologies would provide the most effective support for the library's service priorities, and what technologies would allow the library's administrative functions to be managed more efficiently?" *Technology for Results* was written to address these questions. It provides the tools and processes you need to identify and manage your technology needs today and for the foreseeable future.

Some Basic Definitions

Every public library is a little different. Staff in one library talk about "branches," in another library they use the term "agencies," and in a third the staff refer to both branches and departments as "units." Some libraries have central libraries, others have main libraries. There are libraries that report to authority boards and libraries that are units of the government entity that funds them, which may or not have advisory boards. These differences can cause confusion among readers because each reader expects to see his or her reality reflected in the terms and examples used. The following is a list of basic library terms and their meanings *in this book*:

Branch. A separate library facility.

Central library. The largest library facility, normally in a downtown area; referred to as the "main library" in some places.

Department. A unit within a single facility that is normally a central library.

Library. The entire organizational entity and its units.

Manager. This term is used generically to refer to the staff member or staff members who are responsible for resource allocation in a particular area; in some libraries, the "manager" is actually a team of staff members.

Team. A group of staff members brought together to work on a specific project or program; often includes members from different departments and with different job classifications.

Unit. A term used to refer to individual library departments or branches.

The Tree County Library was introduced in *Staffing for Results* and has appeared in several Results publications. Tree County is a mythical county somewhere in the United States with a countywide population of 400,000 people. The library serves the residents of Tree County with seven branches and has a governing board. You will read more about the Tree County Public Library in the successive parts of the case study placed throughout this book.

Using the Materials in This Book Effectively

Technology for Results is intended to help library managers and boards to develop technology plans that reflect and support the library's service priorities. This clearly implies that before they can use this book effectively, managers and board members must have a clear understanding of what they are trying to accomplish. This book is a part of PLA's Results Series, so there are references throughout the book to library planning documents developed using the *New Planning for Results* process. However, that certainly is not the only process that libraries use to identify priorities. Some libraries have participated in city or county strategic planning processes. Other libraries choose to develop annual goals and objectives for the library as a whole rather than developing a multiyear plan. Still others develop goals and objectives for individual units or for specific programs or services.

What should you do if your library has no current strategic service plan? Must you complete a whole planning process before you can use any of the tools in this book? Absolutely not. *Technology for Results* can be used to develop a technology plan regardless of your environment. However, it is worth repeating that this book is about sustaining, expanding, or adding technologies that support the library's service priorities, not about determining what those service priorities should be. *Before you can decide whether or not your current technological investments are effective and efficient, you must know what you want to accomplish.* Any process used to determine the library's desired outcomes can serve as the starting point for the processes described in this book. More information about determining service priorities is provided in chapter 1.

NOTES

1. Public Library Association Mission Statement, http://www.pla.org/factsheet.html.
2. Sandra Nelson, *The New Planning for Results: A Streamlined Approach* (Chicago: American Library Association, 2001).
3. Sandra Nelson, Ellen Altman, and Diane Mayo, *Managing for Results: Effective Resource Allocation for Public Libraries* (Chicago: American Library Association, 2000).
4. Diane Mayo and Jeanne Goodrich, *Staffing for Results: A Guide to Working Smarter* (Chicago: American Library Association, 2002).
5. Sandra Nelson and June Garcia, *Creating Policies for Results: From Chaos to Clarity* (Chicago: American Library Association, 2003).
6. Diane Mayo and Sandra Nelson, *Wired for the Future: Developing Your Library's Technology Plan* (Chicago: American Library Association, 1999).

Chapter 1

The Planning Process

A typical day for a library staff member starts like this:

Open the back door by keying a code or waving your badge at the electronic security system.

Swing by your desk to boot up your computer before you get your morning coffee, tea, or cola.

Check to make sure the book-drops have been emptied and staff are checking the items in on the integrated library system.

Read and respond to the most urgent e-mail.

Stroll through the public service area to make sure the PCs are on, there is a chair in front of each one, and the printers all have paper.

Check the PC at your service desk to make sure the Internet connection is working.

Smile because the doors just opened and here come the customers.

With variations for local practice, most library staff start their days in similar ways. Technology is such a fundamental tool in twenty-first-century, first-world libraries that we don't even think of much of it as "technology" anymore—unless it is giving us problems. Materials selectors use vendor and commercial websites to identify titles for purchase. The accounting staff use automated systems to cut checks and manage the budget. The board agenda and minutes are written with word-processing software, are sent to the board members via e-mail, and are posted on the library's website in compliance with open meeting laws. Even in the smallest libraries, the director has a PC she uses for word processing and e-mail. And thanks to the Bill and Melinda Gates Library Foundation, nearly every library has at least a few PCs available for public use. Many libraries have dozens or even hundreds of public PC workstations available to support their service delivery.

We no longer discuss whether or not a library *should* invest in technology, but we are still grappling with how much technology we need, how we choose from among the myriad options available, and how we are going to fund it. This book will help you resolve these issues. *Technology for Results* is not about which technologies you should consider buying. Nor does it contain technical information about how to install and utilize various technologies. There are plenty of books written about the technologies themselves, from the basic *For Dummies* series to the highly technical how-to-do-it manuals printed by publishers such as O'Reilly, SAMS, and Microsoft. This book is about the process of identifying what you need to support the library's service objectives and then developing a coherent plan to fund and implement those technological tools.

It All Starts with Service

It is an axiom of the Public Library Association's Results Series that planning for expenditures begins with planning for services. The core book of the series, *The New Planning for Results*, identifies four resources that library managers have at their disposal to achieve their objectives: staff, collections, facilities, and technology. Acquiring each of these resources requires funding. Ensuring that you spend that funding in the most effective way requires linking your spending to your service objectives.[1]

Although it is possible to develop a technology plan without a service plan, it is not recommended. As anyone living in the modern world knows, there are endless opportunities to spend money on technology. The technology planning process explained in this book is designed to help you select from among the options. The only way you can answer the question "Is this a good technology for us to invest in?" is to first determine what services the proposed technology will support. Then you ask: "Are these services my library wants to offer?" Your library's strategic service plan answers this second question. If your library doesn't have a current strategic plan, see figures 2 and 3 for suggestions on how to determine service priorities before moving on.

It is important to acknowledge, however, that a library's technology plan can be affected by more than just the library's service plan. External agencies and actions can impact technology planning, too. A good example of this was the December 2000 passage of the federal Children's Internet Protection Act (CIPA). Libraries that had made a decision to not filter public Internet access were faced with the loss of significant government funding. Many libraries decided to comply with the provisions of CIPA and install

If your library does not have a strategic service plan, you don't have to stop your technology planning until you develop such a plan. You will, however, have to identify some service priorities before you continue.

How Can You Determine Your Service Priorities?

The most effective way for your library to determine its service priorities is to base your discussion on the thirteen public library service responses, which are described in *The New Planning for Results: A Streamlined Approach.* Service responses are defined as "what a library does for, or offers to, the public in an effort to meet a set of well-defined community needs. They represent the gathering and deployment of specific critical resources to produce a specific public benefit or result."

The New Planning for Results provides extensive information about each of these service responses, including the following:

- example of the need addressed
- what the library does and provides
- some possible components
- target audiences and service aspects
- resource allocation issues to consider, further subdivided by staff, collection/information resources, facilities, and technology
- possible measures to consider
- stories describing how real libraries provide the service

Who Will Be Involved in the Selection of Service Responses?

The selection of service responses is not the responsibility of the technology planning committee, although one or more of the committee members may be involved. If service responses must be selected, representatives from the library board, library administration, and the various public service sections of the library should be involved in the selection. The library director will appoint someone to lead that process and will decide who else to involve in the selection process.

How Will the Service Responses Be Selected?

The person managing the process to select service responses will want to read *The New Planning for Results* carefully, paying special attention to the sections that address the service responses. For this very abbreviated process, the service responses can probably be selected in a single meeting. Because service responses are intended to meet specific community needs, it would be helpful to prepare a brief (one- or two-page) profile of the community. The participants should receive a copy of the community profile and a summary of the service responses prior to the meeting.

The meeting will begin with a review of the community profile and a discussion of community needs. The group will then discuss each of the service responses. Finally, the group will select the three to five service responses that most effectively address the identified community needs. There are several suggested processes to help groups reach agreement on service responses included in the Tool Kit section of *The New Planning for Results.*

filtering software. Technology plans that hadn't included filtering were rewritten while library technology support staff figured out how to comply with CIPA.

Another aspect of library operations that affects technology planning is ongoing support for the existing technologies. Every library has some type of technology in place today. Like our book collections, our technology becomes outdated and worn and needs to be replaced. When the worn technology directly supports public service, it is easy to see the link between its replacement and the strategic service plan. But when the worn technology is a staff or backroom item, the need to plan for the upgrade sometimes escapes notice until it becomes a crisis. The first time you discover that your accounting program is so old that you can no longer get the developer to support it often occurs when you are busiest with the budget or end-of-year reports. Planning for the continued

FIGURE 3

Library Service Responses

BASIC LITERACY: A library that offers Basic Literacy service addresses the need to read and to perform other essential daily tasks.

BUSINESS & CAREER INFORMATION: A library that offers Business & Career Information service addresses a need for information related to business, careers, work, entrepreneurship, personal finances, and obtaining employment.

COMMONS: A library that provides a Commons environment helps address the need of people to meet and interact with others in their community and to participate in public discourse about community issues.

COMMUNITY REFERRAL: A library that offers Community Referral addresses the need for information related to services provided by community agencies and organizations.

CONSUMER INFORMATION: A library that provides Consumer Information service helps to satisfy the need for information that impacts the ability of community residents to make informed consumer decisions and to help them become more self-sufficient.

CULTURAL AWARENESS: A library that offers Cultural Awareness service helps satisfy the desire of community residents to gain an understanding of their own cultural heritage and the cultural heritage of others.

CURRENT TOPICS & TITLES: A library that provides Current Topics & Titles helps to fulfill community residents' appetite for information about popular cultural and social trends and their desire for satisfying recreational experiences.

FORMAL LEARNING SUPPORT: A library that offers Formal Learning Support helps students who are enrolled in a formal program of education or who are pursuing their education through a program of home-schooling to attain their educational goals.

GENERAL INFORMATION: A library that offers General Information helps meet the need for information and answers to questions on a broad array of topics related to work, school, and personal life.

GOVERNMENT INFORMATION: The library that offers Government Information service helps satisfy the need for information about elected officials and governmental agencies that enable people to participate in the democratic process.

INFORMATION LITERACY: A library that provides Information Literacy service helps address the need for skills related to finding, evaluating, and using information effectively.

LIFELONG LEARNING: A library that provides Lifelong Learning service helps address the desire for self-directed personal growth and development opportunities.

LOCAL HISTORY & GENEALOGY: A library that offers Local History & Genealogy service addresses the desire of community residents to know and better understand personal or community heritage.

Source: Sandra Nelson, *The New Planning for Results: A Streamlined Approach* (Chicago: American Library Association, 2001), 65.

support of mission-critical existing technologies is just as important as planning for new or improved services.

Content and Infrastructure

The technology-based services offered by libraries generally consist of two elements: content and infrastructure.

Content is electronic information used by staff and the public in the provision of services. Content includes sources of data provided by commercial vendors, as well as data developed by library staff. Examples of content include licensed electronic databases, electronic pathfinders and bibliographies, e-mail marketing pieces such as electronic newsletters, library web pages, digitized photo collections, online event calendars, and a whole host of other sources of data.

Infrastructure is a comprehensive term that encompasses all of the elements required to make electronic *content* and services available to the staff and public. Infrastructure includes the hardware, operating system software and workstation applications, networks, and telecommunications services that support the delivery of your technology-based services and electronic content. Infrastructure elements in a library may include both products you buy (the online library system) and products you simply contract to use (telephone lines or outsourced e-mail services). As technologies and the people who offer and support them change, the buy versus contract decisions can change as well.

In this context, infrastructure also includes the skills it takes to install and operate the technologies you choose to implement. You can also buy or contract for these skills. You buy skills when you hire staff with specific skills or train existing staff in new skills. You contract for skills when you hire a third party to provide you with needed services.

This book deals with planning for the infrastructure needed to deliver content and services to the public and the staff. Content itself is not covered in this book. A number of other publications cover the issues of selecting and licensing electronic content and developing content for library websites.

The Technology Planning Process

Library managers have long recognized the need to have comprehensive selection policies and collection development plans. For centuries, print collections were the core of any library's services. During the twentieth century, the whole public library management structure was organized to provide an infrastructure that supported these collections. Staff were given specific responsibilities for selecting, purchasing, cataloging, processing, displaying, circulating, and shelving printed materials. The bulk of the space in a library building was allocated for shelving to house those materials. The annual budget contained specific line items to support collection maintenance and development. When libraries began adding significant numbers of nonprint items to their traditionally print collections in the 1980s, the collection support infrastructure was modified to address issues specific to the new media, but no fundamental changes were made.

Staff in many libraries tried to use the same traditional collection support infrastructure when they began adding electronic resources to their collections in the mid-1990s. However, it rapidly became apparent that the underlying infrastructure needs for electronic resources and services were very different from those that libraries had traditionally maintained. Books and media are relatively simple to manage—buy them, process them, shelve them. The key piece of "equipment" needed isn't equipment at all; it is shelving, which is one size fits almost all (and many librarians are very cranky about the few oversized books that don't fit) and which often lasts decades once purchased.

Electronic content and services, on the other hand, need to be supported by an extensive and relatively complex infrastructure. To deliver electronic services, libraries need PCs, monitors, keyboards, mice, printers, servers, cables, wiring, connectivity, and more. None of these items is one size fits all and very few last longer than five years. The challenges of managing a technological infrastructure quickly became apparent to library managers who were beginning to provide electronic services. However, few of those managers had the training or the expertise to develop and maintain the infrastructure needed to provide electronic resources and service—and neither did many other librarians. Most library managers had to hire technical staff with little or no library training to manage their technology needs. These technical staff members viewed the library technology as an end in itself—and for those staff members it was. There was no history of integrated planning for technology issues and service issues for either managers or technical staff members to use as a guide in this new environment.

Before 1996, technology planning usually meant asking vendors of integrated library systems to provide cost estimates for a system so the library staff would know how much money to request in the budget to fund a new or upgraded system. Another all too frequent technology "planning" process was applying for grants that would fund technology purchases, often without any clear link between the grantor's objectives and the library's own service objectives. These types of "plans" sometimes resulted in equipment and software that didn't get used. In many cases, programs were initiated that were dropped as soon as the funding ceased because the library had no real commitment to the service.

The need for technology planning became a reality for many libraries with the passage of the Telecommunications Act of 1996. The provisions of this act included funding (known as E-rate funding) to assist libraries with telecommunications costs and the facilities remodeling needed to support networked electronic services. A provision of the bill required libraries to have technology plans in place prior to the award of funds. Early E-rate guidelines did not require that technology plans be linked to library services, which tended to reinforce the feeling that library technology was an end in itself.

In 1997, the Bill and Melinda Gates Library Foundation began to provide hardware, software, training, and support to public libraries in states around the country. The Gates computers were the initial set of networked PCs in many libraries. Foundation staff expected that once library managers saw how popular networked services were, they would plan for and fund the replacement of the first PCs. Unfortunately, in many libraries the Gates computers were not fully integrated into the provision of library services. Instead they were kept apart and used to offer access to educational and office automation software and general Internet surfing. Since they weren't used to provide "real" library services, the need to plan for their replacement was not always obvious to library managers, boards, and funders. The introduction of statewide and consortial funding of electronic content and the development of service-oriented library web pages and information sites made accessible through the Gates-provided PCs made these groups begin to see the PCs as integral to library service. That, in turn, led to an increased understanding of the importance of technology planning.

The annual or biennial budget cycle, the need to produce "approved" annual plans for E-rate funding, and even the earlier Results Series book *Wired for the Future: Developing Your Library Technology Plan* suggest it is sufficient to treat a technology planning process as an event to be undertaken annually at most, or even less frequently if possible. But library technology staff know that long-term plans are often changed by near-term requirements. As noted earlier, the Children's Internet Protection Act was passed in 2000 and some libraries complied with its requirements that year. In other libraries, the management team and board decided to wait until all of the legal appeals concerning the act were complete. In June 2003, the Supreme Court ruled that CIPA was constitutional, and this meant that many library staff found themselves spending the 2003–2004 budget year grappling with CIPA-imposed filtering in order to continue receiving federal E-rate funds despite the existence of other planned technology implementations.

This book will describe a process for developing a technology plan as a planning event for libraries that do not have an existing technology plan. But it will end with a suggested strategy for maintaining the technology plan as an active, flexible, continually refreshed document that is reviewed and adjusted as needed to respond to internal and external changes.

Tasks in the Technology Planning Process

A technology plan is a plan for acquiring and expanding technology-related resources. It is about filling the gap between what you have available to achieve your service objectives and what you determine you need to achieve those objectives.[2] To do this you need

- an inventory of the elements of your current technology infrastructure; and
- projections of the technology infrastructure you will require to support planned services or improved productivity.

The difference between what you have and what you need is what you plan to get. Sounds simple, right?

Of course, it is not that simple. Technology planning is not just about new services. Library managers need to plan for sustaining, modifying, or expanding current programs as well as implementing new ones. Vendors cease support for older equipment, and you have to plan for its replacement. Older hardware and operating systems won't run the software you need, so upgrades become necessary. Of course, this is not so different from our continuous purchasing of new materials to replenish popular, well-used circulating collections. But most librarians learned how to think about collection development in library school, and most have participated in some aspect of collection development all of their professional lives. By contrast, many of us had no formal training in developing our library's technological infrastructure; we are learning by doing.

This book recommends a set of ten tasks to undertake—by yourself, with a few other staff, or as a committee effort—that will lead you through the process of developing and implementing a technology plan. (See figure 4.) While the book focuses on a committee approach, it is important to realize that the process can be done even in a library with a

---

FIGURE 4
Ten Tasks for Technology Planning

Task 1   Identify Results

Task 2   Choose the Committee

Task 3   Evaluate Existing Services

Task 4   Identify New Services

Task 5   Assess the Current Technology Environment

Task 6   Determine the Requirements of New or Expanded Services

Task 7   Select and Present

Task 8   Inform

Task 9   Implement the Projects in the Plan

Task 10 Sustain the Planning Process

---

small staff. The tasks are the same even when you have only yourself or one or two other staff members to consult.

Where to Begin

Before you initiate a technology planning process in your library, ask yourself what you need to get out of the effort. What do you need to know at the end of the planning process? What results are you expecting? And who, other than yourself, will need to see, use, or review the technology plan?

The answers to these questions will vary widely depending on your internal and external operating environments. A technology plan can range from a general description of the changes or additions you will make to your technological infrastructure to support specific services you intend to deliver ("the library will revamp its website to provide easier, more intuitive access to all of its electronic resources") to a detailed set of implementation steps, each with a timeline and an associated cost. The more detailed you become, the more labor-intensive the planning process will be.

You don't want to spend more time on developing your technology plan than you need to. But you should recognize that the planning process can serve more purposes than simply listing the hardware and software you want to buy. The planning process can spark conversation about the ways technology might support more efficient operations, which can lead to rethinking workflows. The planning process can provide a forum for technology staff and services staff to jointly design technology-based services, breaking down any "them versus us" barriers that might exist. It can even jump-start better project management by focusing as much attention on *how* to implement the technology plan as it does on *what* technologies to adopt.

If your technology funding is a part of the operational budget and needs little justification, then a plan that simply outlines the library's priorities and expected timetables may be all you need. Many smaller libraries that participate in technology consortia acquire all of their technology through their consortium membership fees and depend entirely on the consortium's staff for implementation and support services. For these libraries, it makes sense to develop local plans based on the consortium's plan, linking the larger group's plan to local needs. Describing the services to be offered and providing information on when new or expanded services are expected to be available may well be a sufficient plan.

Consortium members that offer technology services beyond those supported by the consortium and libraries with staff that manage their own technology environments generally will want a more detailed plan. Libraries that are a part of city or county government may have specific technology planning requirements that their parent organizations impose. Libraries that intend to file their plans with their state library in compliance with E-rate requirements need to be sure to include all the necessary elements.[3] Thinking about what you need the plan to include and who will use it helps to ensure that the results of your effort will meet all your needs.

All of the tasks and steps in the technology planning process are detailed in figure 5. As you work through the tasks and steps, you will find that you have options at various points in the process, and your choices will depend on the planning results you identify at the beginning of the process.

FIGURE 5
Technology Planning Process

Task 1: Identify Results

Step 1.1   Identify the audiences
Step 1.2   Identify the technology planning results
Step 1.3   Determine the planning timeline

Task 2: Choose the Committee

Step 2.1   Appoint a committee chair
Step 2.2   Select staff for the committee
Step 2.3   Consider the role of outsiders
Step 2.4   Provide an orientation for the committee

Task 3: Evaluate Existing Services

Step 3.1   Develop an inventory of current technology-supported services
Step 3.2   Match existing technologies and services to the strategic service plan
Step 3.3   Decide which existing technologies and services should be sustained, expanded, or phased out

Task 4: Identify New Services

Step 4.1   Identify opportunities for more effective public services through technology projects
Step 4.2   Identify opportunities for more efficient or effective administrative functioning through technology projects
Step 4.3   Evaluate options
Step 4.4   Create a list of technology projects to sustain, expand, phase out, and add
Step 4.5   Make a preliminary presentation to the library administration

Task 5: Assess the Current Technology Environment

Step 5.1   Assess future upgrades or replacement requirements for existing infrastructure to sustain services
Step 5.2   Assess staff skills
Step 5.3   Develop cost estimates for upgrades or replacements needed to sustain current services

Task 6: Determine the Requirements of New or Expanded Services

Step 6.1   Determine technical infrastructure, skills requirements, and costs for expanded or new services
Step 6.2   Identify available staff resources with the necessary skills
Step 6.3   Develop time estimates for each project or pilot as needed

Task 7: Select and Present

Step 7.1   Begin with needed investments to sustain current levels of service
Step 7.2   Choose from among expansion and new projects
Step 7.3   Write up decisions with rationale and anticipated outcomes; provide estimated budgets and timelines
Step 7.4   Present as needed to decision makers for approval and commitment to funding

Task 8: Inform

Step 8.1   Present the adopted plan to target audiences
Step 8.2   Inform the public

(cont.)

FIGURE 5
Technology Planning Process *(cont.)*

Task 9: Implement the Projects in the Plan

Step 9.1   Identify a project sponsor for each implementation
Step 9.2   Identify a project manager and develop a projected timeline with needed resources
Step 9.3   Plan a data-capture strategy to measure success
Step 9.4   Report regularly on progress to all
Step 9.5   Capture and use trigger points for assessment of later implementations

Task 10: Sustain the Planning Process

Step 10.1   Measure and report results
Step 10.2   Update the infrastructure inventory
Step 10.3   Update the services inventory

TASK 1: IDENTIFY RESULTS

Task 1: Identify Results
> **Step 1.1: Identify the audiences.**
> **Step 1.2: Identify the technology planning results.**
> **Step 1.3: Determine the planning timeline.**

Task 2: Choose the Committee

Task 3: Evaluate Existing Services

Task 4: Identify New Services

Task 5: Assess the Current Technology Environment

Task 6: Determine the Requirements of New or Expanded Services

Task 7: Select and Present

Task 8: Inform

Task 9: Implement the Projects in the Plan

Task 10: Sustain the Planning Process

Identifying the results for the planning process starts by identifying the audiences for the plan. Who will need to review, approve, or understand the plan? The board? Staff who will use the selected technologies? External funders? Library budget planners? Each group you identify will have its own specific information needs. The key to determining the results you want to achieve is to understand what those needs are. If you identify the information the audiences will want at the start, you can be sure the plan includes all the information you will need when you get to Tasks 7 and 8, the tasks where you get needed approvals and inform everyone of the plan.

Step 1.1
Identify the Audiences

Use Workform 1, Audiences and Planning Results, to list the audiences you expect to be affected by the plan in some way. Then ask yourself what you want or expect each audience to do as a result of the plan. The board may have to act on some of the plan's recommendations to provide needed funding. Line staff will actually be implementing parts of the technology plan, so they need to have an idea of when the changes are going to occur and what kind of training will be provided to support new or expanded services. You want the budget folks to support the plan, so they may need the costs and some timelines. Figure 6 depicts a typical example of Workform 1.

FIGURE 6

Example of Workform 1, Audiences and Planning Results

A. Audience	B. Inform (I) or Participate (P)	C. Need to Know
Board	I	Services to be delivered Costs
County Information Technology Department	P	Equipment to be purchased
State Library/E-Rate	I	Services to be delivered Professional development plans Needed equipment, software, and telecommunications Costs Evaluation criteria
Staff	P	Services to be delivered Timeline Training plans
Library Managers	I	Services to be delivered Timeline Costs

PLANNING RESULTS

The Tree County Public Library technology plan should be a blueprint to improve services through the use of technology. It must

- identify what services we will offer
- identify what additional investments we need to make to achieve our service goals
- include training for staff
- establish realistic goals for implementation that support budget planning
- include ways to measure results

This is also a good time to begin to think about the role each audience should have in the development of the plan. A few of the audiences you identify will simply need to be informed about the plan but will not need to participate in the development of the plan itself. Other audiences, especially the staff, maybe the board, and possibly external audiences such as city or county IT (information technology) staff, may need to be involved as the technology plan is developed.

A technology planning process is an opportunity to build consensus among the groups who will be affected by your plan. Think about whether or not the audiences you identify can be advocates for the plan with others; if so, involving them from the start would be a way to build support. Conversely, if an identified audience has the ability to veto or derail the plan, then it is important to involve members of that group from the start to ensure that any objections they may have are addressed in the planning process.

Participation in the technology planning process can range from attendance at every meeting and active involvement in each task to offering review and comment opportunities along the way. After you appoint a chairperson for the planning effort, discuss your thoughts on participation with that person. Supporters are always welcome, but critics should be welcomed as well. One key to managing potential opposition is to ensure that critics can't say "No one asked me about this."

Step 1.2
Identify the Planning Results

After you have determined the audiences for the technology plan, decided what you want them to do with the plan, and defined what they need to know, you are ready to identify the technology planning results you intend to achieve. These will be used to create the charge given to the technology planning committee. The list of your intended results, taken together, should create a clear picture of what you expect the technology planning committee to produce. As noted earlier, for some libraries, the committee charge will be quite limited, while for other libraries the charge will be detailed and comprehensive. The charge for your committee will depend on the unique circumstances in your library.

Look at the Need to Know column of Workform 1. This is the list of the data elements that need to be included in the technology plan. Now look at the Planning Results part of the workform. The process of developing the technology planning results gives you the chance to communicate your own vision of the role that technology should play in your library. In the example shown in figure 6, the planning results begin with "The Tree County Public Library technology plan should be a blueprint to improve services through the use of technology." This lets the planning committee know that the plan they produce should be linked to the library's service objectives.

You will want to involve your senior staff in the development of the technology planning results and in the identification of the audiences for your plan. Senior staff themselves are an important audience for the technology plan; they need to know what the process will be and how it will affect their departments and staff. They can be helpful in surfacing issues and questions that staff will have about the process, and they may be able to identify additional audiences or information needs.

Step 1.3
Determine the Planning Timeline

How long should the planning process take? As mentioned earlier, the ideal technology planning environment is not a onetime event, but rather a continuous process of periodic review, with ongoing adjustments made as services evolve and external forces affect the library's technology environment. Creating the initial plan from which you can begin this periodic review should take no more than four to five months. (See figure 7, Example of Technology Planning Timeline.)

FIGURE 7

Example of Technology Planning Timeline

Task	Action	Date
Tasks 1 and 2	Develop the Planning Process • Identify audiences for the plan • Appoint a committee chair • Write the planning objective • Select committee members • Develop the planning timeline • Consider the role of outsiders	Month One
Step 2.4	Orientation Meeting for the Committee • Review audiences and objectives • Review suggested timeline	Month Two
Task 3	Evaluate Existing Services • Develop inventory of technology-supported services • Match existing technologies and services to the strategic service plan • Make sustain, expand, or phase out decisions	
Task 4	Identify New Services • Identify opportunities • Evaluate options • Create list of new projects to consider	
Task 5	Assess the Current Technology Environment • Develop inventories of current hardware, software, networks, and skills • Assess future upgrades or replacement requirements for existing infrastructure to sustain services • Develop cost estimates for upgrades or replacements needed to sustain current services	Month Three
Task 6	Determine the Requirements of New or Expanded Services • Determine technical infrastructure, skills requirements, and costs for expanded or new services • Identify available staff resources with necessary skills • Develop time estimates for each project	
Task 7	Select and Present • Select projects • Write up decisions with rationale and anticipated outcomes; provide estimated budgets and timelines • Present as needed to decision makers for approval	Month Four
Task 8	Inform • Present plan to target audiences • Inform the public	
Task 9	Implement the Projects in the Plan • Identify a sponsor for each project • Identify a project manager and develop projected timeline • Plan a data-capture strategy • Report regularly on progress	Month Five
Task 10	Sustain the Planning Process • Measure and report results • Update the infrastructure and service inventories	Ongoing

As you will see when you get to Task 6, Determine Requirements, sometimes simply determining the requirements to implement a desired technology is a project in itself. This means that the technology plan you develop using the processes described in this book may identify issues that cannot be resolved immediately and will include the future dates on which you expect to have enough information to resolve those issues. But moving through the first five tasks (Identify Results, Choose the Committee, Evaluate Existing Services, Identify New Services, and Assess Technology) and setting firm dates for Task 6 (Determine Requirements) and Task 7 (Select and Present) should be doable in four to five months. Task 8 (Inform) and Task 9 (Implement the Projects in the Plan) are implementation tasks and will go on throughout the life of your technology plan. Task 10 (Sustain the Planning Process) describes how to move into continuous review and regular updating of your technology plan rather than waiting for two or three years and then initiating a whole new planning process.

A good technology plan incorporates the input of the public services staff who provide direct services to the public, the support staff who use technology to manage in-house functions, and the technology staff who are directly responsible for maintaining the library's technological infrastructure. The public services and support staff members bring their perspective as users of the technology to the planning process. These staff members can often see ways in which their job performance can be improved through technology applications. Public services staff have the most direct contact with library users and can often articulate ways in which existing technology can be improved or new technologies can be employed in order to enhance services.

But public services and support staff are often unaware of the requirements of implementing new or enhanced technologies. The technology staff's input is crucial here in tempering "great ideas" with the reality of what it will take to actually make those ideas come alive. Technology staff also understand the level of maintenance needed in the existing infrastructure. They know all too well the problems of maintaining old equipment and protecting the library's technical environment from viruses, hackers, and accidents. Technology staff are aware of when equipment and software have reached—or are about to reach—the "end of life" and are no longer supported by the manufacturers or developers.

These different perspectives of the public service staff, the support staff, and the technology staff are important in developing a technology plan. Each group has a specific role to play in the process. Public service staff and support staff can articulate needs, technology staff can figure out how to "make it so," and all staff members can work together to envision the future. Of course, there are times when the technology staff have to say that the skills or tools simply don't exist in the organization to achieve the dreams. In that case all of the staff need to work together to determine how much of the dream is possible with the available resources. A good technology planning environment is one in which the public services staff, support staff, and technology staff are continuously passing ideas back and forth, refining their varied visions into possible results.

TASK 2: CHOOSE THE COMMITTEE

Step 2.1
Appoint a Committee Chair

The most important committee appointment to be made is the committee chair. The chair needs to be someone who has good people skills and a track record of successfully managing projects. He or she should also be capable of managing effective communications between groups and helping diverse groups reach consensus. The committee chair should be familiar with technology issues and with library technology applications, although he or she certainly doesn't need to have the greatest technical expertise on the committee.

It is very likely that the committee chair will be a staff member, although there may be instances in which a board member would be an effective chair. In small and medium-sized libraries, the chair may be the library director. In larger libraries, the chair will probably be someone other than the director. Once the planning committee chair has been appointed, the library director and the chair (if different) will work together to make the rest of the committee appointments.

Step 2.2
Select Staff for the Committee

Technology planning is a process that should involve a wide spectrum of stakeholders throughout your library. It is not a task that you should assign solely to the technology staff "because they are the only ones who understand it." The planning process needs to include people who understand the library's mission and its service objectives. Staff who will use the technologies you select and staff who understand the library's diverse clientele and the way current services and programs are being used need to be included.

You will be selecting your committee members from among the library's public services staff, support staff, technical services staff, and administrative staff, and they will bring different information and strengths to the process. Even if you are in a small library with three or four people serving all of the aforementioned functions, you will still find that each person has specialized skills and interests. In a large library, you will probably have two groups working on your plan: the appointed committee and the staff of the technology department, who will both gather data and work with the data generated by the appointed committee at interim steps along the way. Choose a technology staffer for membership on the appointed committee who can communicate effectively about technology with those who are less familiar with technology issues.

You will want to strike a balance between including representatives of every area in the library and appointing a committee so large that it has difficulty finding times to meet and making decisions. Many public libraries have staff members with specific areas of expertise. The staff from the section serving special populations may know a lot about adaptive technology for the visually or hearing-impaired; staff working with children will be very familiar with software for children; and staff working with periodicals will have expertise in that area. It is not necessary for all of these people to serve as members of the committee for them to participate in the planning process. They can be asked to make presentations to the committee or to attend meetings in which their areas of expertise are being discussed.

Step 2.3
Consider the Role of Outsiders

Look again at the copy of Workform 1 you completed. You have probably included a number of audiences other than the library staff and board. There may be a role in the technology planning process for members of these audiences as well. For example, staff from other city or county IT departments may have more expertise in some areas than the staff in your library's technology department—and will almost certainly have more expertise than any library staff members in a library that doesn't have a technology staff. You may also find outside consultants helpful at points along the way,

When considering whether you want to include non-staff members in the planning process, start by deciding what their role in the process will be. In most cases this will be driven by the skills that your staff representatives bring to the committee. If your staff is not good at envisioning new ways to do work or provide services, you may find an outsider's perspective valuable. If your staff has limited technical expertise, then you may want to include someone who understands what resources are available in your community to implement and support technical projects.

If you decide you need outside assistance, you then have to find that assistance. How you proceed will be based on the resources available to pay for the assistance. If, like most public libraries, you have limited resources, you may want to use the wide variety of free or very inexpensive technical or expert assistance that is available. Sources of general technical assistance include

>   technical or computer support staff of your city or county government
>   technical or computer support staff at one of the local schools or from the school district office
>   local software or hardware users groups

For library-specific expert assistance, consider these resources:

>   state library consultants
>   systemwide or regional library consultants
>   resource-sharing consortium staff members
>   other library directors in libraries approximately your size
>   technical or computer support staff in the larger public libraries in your state
>   local school librarians (if the school library media center has successfully integrated technology into its programs)
>   local community college or college librarians

support personnel from software vendors

representatives from your automation vendor if you already
have an online system and are not planning to replace that system
in the near future

Most libraries also have access to a number of people who will provide free or inexpensive assistance with your planning process. They include

local college or community college professors

county extension personnel

principals or school superintendents

local guidance counselors

local clergy

regional or state library staff

If you have the necessary funds, you may want to hire a specialist in library technology issues or library planning to work with the planning committee. In most cases this will require that you develop and issue a Request for Proposal (RFP). Your local government probably has a format for RFPs. If not, your state library agency may be able to send you one or two samples from other libraries in the state.

It is sometimes difficult to know how to notify potential consultants that you are ready to issue an RFP. Some library consultants advertise their contact information and areas of expertise at www.libraryconsultants.org. Another way to reach consultants is to publish a notice of your RFP in *Library Hotline*, which is read by many consultants, or post notice of your RFP on PUBLIB or one of the other library electronic discussion lists. A number of organizations, including three divisions of the American Library Association—the Library Information and Technology Association, the Library Administration and Management Association, and the Association of Specialized and Cooperative Agencies—publish lists of consultants, with their areas of specialties. These can be obtained by calling the appropriate organization. The Urban Libraries Council also publishes a list of recommended consultants for its members. You might also want to talk to your colleagues in other libraries to see if they can recommend one or more consultants.

Step 2.4
Provide an Orientation for the Committee

The first meeting of the planning committee should be an orientation meeting. The committee orientation has three purposes: (1) you want to ensure that all of the committee members understand the *Technology for Results* process; (2) you want to ensure that all of the committee members have a common understanding of current library operations; and (3) you want everyone to have a common framework for discussing library technology issues. Unless one or more of your committee members has used this manual before, you can assume that all of your committee members will need to be introduced to *Technology for Results*. It may not be as easy to determine what constitutes a common understanding of library technology and current library operations.

WHAT DOES THE COMMITTEE NEED TO KNOW?

Before you can design the orientation for the committee, you have to determine precisely what they need to know. It will probably be easiest to start by defining the minimum that the committee members will need to know about current library practices. When you selected the committee members, you looked at their areas of expertise and tried to ensure that the committee included people who are familiar with library technology and with current library operations. Now you need to look at the individual committee members. Are all of them also library staff members? If so, any orientation you provide about current library operations will be very different than it would be if the committee included city or county staff members and community members. For a staff committee, the minimum base information might include current use statistics, a copy of the current budget, a copy of the strategic plan, and a brief overview of the library's current technology-based services and programs. If your committee includes city or county staff and community members, you will want to broaden that to include information on the library's governance, the number of branches the library has, the number and classifications of staff members, and a brief overview of current services and programs.

HOW CAN YOU PROVIDE THE INFORMATION
THE COMMITTEE NEEDS TO KNOW?

To ensure that all of the committee members hear the same thing at the same time, you will want to schedule a formal orientation meeting. The orientation meeting will probably take two to four hours, depending on the makeup of the committee and the amount of basic information they need about the library.

The first step in the orientation is to explain the *Technology for Results* process to the committee members. It is imperative for the committee chair to have a copy of this manual, and it would be good if other committee members could each have one as well. After you have provided an overview of the process, you will want to distribute copies of the completed Workform 1, Audiences and Planning Results. Encourage the committee to discuss the information on the workform and to suggest revisions or changes.

The second part of the orientation process will focus on the library. All the members of the committee should receive a copy of the library service plan during the orientation. Then someone (the director, the chair of the committee that developed the library service plan, or the technology committee chair) should review the major points in the plan. The committee members should have a general understanding of the library's goals, objectives, major activities, and resource allocation priorities. Many of the decisions that will be made during the technology planning process will be driven by the service priorities in your library service plan. It is critical that all of the committee members understand those priorities.

The third part of the orientation will address technology issues. Start by asking each member of the committee to briefly discuss his or her area of technology expertise. Then ask someone who is well versed in technology *and* is able to discuss technology issues in easily understood terms to lead a general discussion of the current state of library technology and of general technology trends. It would be very helpful if you could send the committee members one or more articles on these issues before the orientation meeting. You may find such articles by checking some of the resources in Appendix A, Identifying Technology Options.

It is clear that the members of this committee will need to develop and maintain a broad understanding of the technologies that affect libraries in order to complete the planning process and that this general introduction only scratches the surface of what they will need to know. Does that mean that you have to postpone the process for six months or a year while the members learn everything they can? Absolutely not. The planning process in which you are all involved will be a significant learning experience. As you explore the options open to the library and discuss the ramifications of those options, you will be developing the foundation for a broad understanding of the technology you need.

Before adjourning the orientation meeting, encourage the committee members to begin to do some study on their own. Finally, assure the committee that if they identify areas in which they need more information as they go through the planning process, short mini-orientation programs can be scheduled to provide the requested information as needed.

What's Next?

You have identified the results you want to achieve through the technology planning process, selected staff and others to serve on the technology planning committee, and provided the committee members with an orientation. The committee members have a clear understanding of their responsibilities. The audiences for the plan and the data elements that need to be included to meet the information needs of those audiences have been identified. The preparation tasks are completed; it is time to begin gathering data about the current library services that are supported by technology and to discuss what new technology might be needed to support the library's public service priorities.

Part 1 of the Tree County Public Library case study illustrates that portion of the planning process discussed in this chapter.

CASE STUDY

TREE COUNTY PUBLIC LIBRARY

PART 1

The Planning Process: Target Audiences and Objectives

The Tree County Public Library has a new director. When she arrived, the library had a recently revised strategic service plan but no written technology plan. In her first six months, the director has learned that the public services staff are frustrated by what they say is the technology support staff's inability to get projects done on time. Staff also feel that their suggestions for new projects are never implemented, that all project suggestions have to originate in the information technology (IT) department if they are to get done.

The head of the IT department tells a different story. She says her department does the best it can, but they are often the last to know when the library will be getting new hardware or software. Grant requests are written without IT input, and staff members purchase and load new software without letting IT know. Everything that is sent to IT from the departments or branches is a "priority rush." The IT staff is feeling overwhelmed and burned out.

The director wants to lower the frustration level and get a handle on all the ways technology is being used in the Tree County Public Library. She also wants the board to approve a line item in the operating budget for technology rather than funding each technology implementation as a special project or with grant funds. She has decided that the best way to achieve these results is to have the staff develop a written technology plan.

The two primary audiences she has identified are the staff and the board. The staff are to be participants, while the board will be informed at the start and end of the planning project, with brief updates along the way. The results she sets for the plan are:

> The Tree County Public Library technology plan should support systemwide service priorities and efficient, cost-effective library operations. It must link our technologies with our services and ensure that all staff have the skills they need to assist customers as they use those services. The plan will guide us in setting budgets and timelines for our technology investments.

The director asks the assistant director to lead the planning team. She is well respected by the staff and has team-building skills. She's not the most technically savvy member of the staff, but she manages conflict well and runs an effective meeting, both skills the director believes will be important.

Together the director and assistant director discuss the other members of the team. They agree on the head of IT and the head of adult services, who is the IT department's most vocal critic. The assistant director also suggests adding the IT department's server and network administrator because he has the most technical skills in the department. A branch manager, the head of children's services, the acquisitions manager, and two senior circulation clerks, one from the main library and one from a branch, round out the group. They agree that the assistant director will talk with the county's IT director about the planning process to determine if there are any county standards or initiatives the library needs to be aware of in its planning process.

Planning Committee Orientation

At the first meeting of the technology planning committee, the director explains the results she expects the committee to achieve. She tells the committee that she has reviewed the current technology budget and the budgets for the past several years, and she thinks an annual technology budget of approximately $75,000, not including IT staff salaries, is a reasonable goal for the Tree County Library. She expects to have the committee's recommendations before the start of the next budget cycle in five months.

The assistant director passes out copies of *Technology for Results* and reviews the ten tasks in the planning process, with particular emphasis on Tasks 3–6, the assessment and recommendation steps.

The group discusses the timeline and agrees to complete the inventory of technology-dependent services and staff skills at the same time. Six members agree to inventory services, while two accept responsibility for inventorying staff skills. All the members agree to look at the list of technology-related skills to be inventoried before the survey goes out and to make suggestions as needed. The target date for completion of these inventories and decisions about current services (sustain, expand, or phase out) is set for four weeks from that day.

Everyone agrees that discussions with the staff on new or improved technology-related services should start immediately and that all committee members will do it. After some discussion, they decide that committee members will schedule at least one meeting with each unit or section in the library to ensure that all staff will have a chance to participate in the planning process. The target completion date for this is also four weeks.

Weeks 5 through 11 will be devoted to assessing the current infrastructure and gathering vendor and cost data on possible new technologies. In week 12, the committee will make choices about its final recommendations and begin to write up those recommendations. By week 14, the written recommendations will go to library administration for review and discussion of the funding requirements. In week 16, library administration will review the draft plan and make any changes or revisions. The board presentation will be scheduled for week 18 with formal adoption by week 20, in time for the budget planning process.

NOTES

1. "Efficiency can be defined as *doing something right* and effectiveness can be defined as *doing the right thing*" (Sandra Nelson, Ellen Altman, and Diane Mayo, *Managing for Results: Effective Resource Allocation for Public Libraries* [Chicago: American Library Association, 2000], 16).
2. A detailed discussion of the gap analysis process can be found in Sandra Nelson, *The New Planning for Results: A Streamlined Approach* (Chicago: American Library Association, 2001), 104–13.
3. Criteria for an approved technology plan can be found on the Universal Service Administration Company website, http://www.sl.universalservice.org/reference/TechnologyPlanningFAQ.asp.

Chapter 2

Identify

MILESTONES

By the time you finish this chapter you will know how to

- identify all the services currently being supported by technology in your library
- make decisions on which technologies should be sustained, expanded, or phased out
- identify opportunities for new technology projects that meet the library's needs
- make choices among the options available

Every library has a variety of technologies installed in it now. To do their work well, the members of the planning committee need to understand this current technology environment. A brief discussion of the library's current technologies was probably held during the planning committee's orientation meeting. Now it is time to review a much more detailed list of the technologies in the library. This will probably start with the library technology inventory or the list of the hardware the library owns or operates, but this will not be all that is required. The committee will also need to understand who benefits from the technology and what public services and administrative functions the technology supports.

Activities supported by library technologies typically fall into one of two categories: public services and administrative functions.

Public service technologies are the ones most easily linked to your strategic service plan. They are the technologies that are used directly by the public or by the staff in serving the public, either in the library or remotely. Examples of direct public service technologies include public access PCs, the library's online integrated system, authentication for access to electronic resources, 24/7 virtual reference, customer self-charge stations, and a whole host of other customer-oriented tools.

Adtrative function technologies are tools used by the staff in the performance of their jobs. Although using these technologies often results in the creation or support of services for the public, the purpose of the technology is to enable staff to do their jobs. Examples of this category of technologies include OCLC cataloging workstations, word processing, e-mail, accounting systems, desktop publishing, and web authoring tools.

Some administrative function tools are selected because they can increase operational efficiency or improve productivity by reducing the amount of time or effort it takes to accomplish a task or by removing barriers to effective performance. A spam filter that reduces the daily barrage of e-mail is an example of a technology that could improve performance by reducing the amount of time it takes to manage e-mail. Using electronic time sheets rather than depending on payroll staff to add up handwritten time sheets is another example.

Of course, a number of technologies used by libraries fit into more than one category. A PC in a branch workroom, for example, is often used for multiple purposes, e.g., to check e-mail, write memos, select materials, and check in books. A PC on the reference desk in that same branch is probably also used to check e-mail on occasion. The workroom PC is primarily a staff tool used to support administrative functions and is occasionally used for public service (checking in books), while the reference desk PC is primarily a public service technology that is occasionally used for an administrative purpose. As you go through the planning process, you will be asked to designate the *primary* use of your technologies because you will use different criteria in judging whether or not to expand an existing public service or administrative function.

TASK 3: EVALUATE EXISTING SERVICES

Task 1: Identify Results

Task 2: Choose the Committee

Task 3: Evaluate Existing Services

    Step 3.1: Develop an inventory of current technology-supported services.

    Step 3.2: Match existing technologies and services to the strategic service plan.

    Step 3.3: Decide which existing technologies and services should be sustained, expanded, or phased out.

Task 4: Identify New Services

Task 5: Assess the Current Technology Environment

Task 6: Determine the Requirements of New or Expanded Services

Task 7: Select and Present

Task 8: Inform

Task 9: Implement the Projects in the Plan

Task 10: Sustain the Planning Process

Throughout the *Technology for Results* process there will be several points at which the committee or the library's technology support staff will be dealing with the library's inventory of currently installed equipment and software. The first such point is when using the inventory of what is installed as the basis for creating a list of currently supported services.

Step 3.1
Develop an Inventory of Current Technology-Supported Services

Technology planning is not just about adding new services or functions. A critical component of good technology management is ensuring continued support for existing successful services and necessary administrative functions. You will begin the planning process by charging committee members with the responsibility to develop a list of technology-supported services and functions currently available in your library. This process will help familiarize the committee members with the current technical environment in your library.

Although the end result will be a list of technology-supported services and functions, the easiest way to identify all of them is to start with a list of the hardware that is presently installed and then link each item on that list to the services or functions that it supports. This approach serves the dual purpose of making sure you identify all current technology-supported services and administrative functions and that you uncover all of the existing equipment, even that which might no longer be actively in use.

Begin the services inventory with a list of the installed desktop workstations, servers, and other technologies such as scanners, self-check machines, and printers in your library.[1] Every library should have such a list of hardware indicating where each item is installed. If such a list doesn't exist in your library, see Appendix B, Developing a Technical Inventory, for information on how to develop a technical inventory.

Workform 2, Services Inventory, provides a form for collecting and recording the services and functions that are linked to the items on your physical inventory list. If your library's technical inventory is in a machine-readable format such as an Excel spreadsheet or an Access database, consider copying the file and adding columns or fields to record the service information on the workform. You can then use a printout of the data to record what you discover as you work through the inventory of services rather than using Workform 2.

Committee members will complete a copy of the workform for each unit of the library. They will enter a descriptive name for each PC or group of PCs in column A of the form and the total number of PCs in that group in column B. In column C, they will indicate whether the PCs are used primarily for public services (PS) or administrative functions (AF). Finally, in column D they will make a brief note of the primary services or functions supported by the PCs. (Figure 8 shows a completed portion of Workform 2.)

FIGURE 8
Example of Workform 2, Services Inventory

Location: Elm Branch

PART 2: PC Workstations

A. Equipment	B. No.	C. PS or AF	D. Services Delivered
Adult public Internet station	4	PS	Internet access—by reservation
Adult public Internet station	2	PS	Internet—15-minute limit, no reservation
CD-ROM tower	1	PS	Access to periodical databases
Staff workroom PC	1	AF	Staff e-mail and word processing
Branch manager's PC	1	AF	Assorted administrative stuff

WHERE CAN YOU GET THE INFORMATION?

The best way to get this information is to ask how each device in the inventory is being used. If the technology planning committee includes a member from each of your service units (sections, departments, or branches), each of these persons can be charged with completing Workform 2, Services Inventory, for his or her unit. If you have more units than committee members, some committee members will have to be responsible for gathering information in more than one unit. Note that Workform 2 includes more than just a list of the devices. It asks you to determine what services or functions each device is supporting. This is the primary purpose of the workform. The list of devices is just the mechanism for gathering this data.

Remind the committee members that they can't assume they know how a workstation is being used simply because they know how it is supposed to be used, particularly if it is a staff workstation. Even if your library controls the software on PCs to the point where staff are not allowed to download new programs, the myriad of software available on most staff PCs provides for a wide range of uses. Encourage committee members to make it their business to understand how the PCs are actually being used. They will need to talk to the staff who use or oversee the equipment and ask them questions. Many operational inefficiencies develop because creative, dedicated staff "make do" with technologies that don't quite meet their needs. For instance, in some libraries branch managers do not have access to the budget subsystem of the integrated library system's acquisitions module, so they develop their own Excel spreadsheets to track expenditures. A good technology planning process will ferret out these issues and address them.

SUMMARIZE THE INFORMATION

When the committee members have completed the services inventory for each unit, the committee chair or a designated committee member will be responsible for summarizing all of the information from column D of all of the completed copies of Workform 2 in column A (Service) of Workform 3, Strategic Plan Links, or column A (Function) of Workform 4, Administrative Tools. Remember, the purpose of completing Workform 2 was to identify *services*, which were noted in column D. You started from the list of equipment to ensure that you didn't skip any services. You will be using the equipment list later in the process, but right now your focus is on *how* the equipment is being used—your technology-supported services or functions.

Use Workform 3, Strategic Plan Links, to summarize information about the services identified as public service (PS) in column B of Workform 2. To complete column A of Workform 3, enter each identified service from column D of Workform 2 on its own line. When you are done transcribing data from the Workform 2s to Workform 3, you will have a full list of the technology-supported public services the library is offering today in column A. (See figure 9.)

The entries identified on Workform 2 as administrative functions or basic business tools (AF) will be transcribed to column A of Workform 4, Administrative Tools, entering each identified function on its own line in the workform. The completed Workform 4 provides a list of the administrative functions supported by technology in your library. (See figure 10.)

FIGURE 9

Workform 3, Strategic Plan Links—Example 1

A. Service	B. Strategic Plan Links or Admin/Staff	C. Sustain (S) Expand (E) Phase Out (P)
Adult Internet access— by reservation		
Adult Internet access— 15 minutes; no reservation		
CD-ROM periodical databases		

FIGURE 10

Example of Workform 4, Administrative Tools

A. Function	B. Sustain (S) Expand (E) Phase Out (P)
Branch manager administrative stuff	
Staff e-mail and word processing	

The data on Workform 3 and Workform 4 provide the basis for the next step in the process, during which the committee will get together and make some preliminary decisions about the current technology environment.

Step 3.2
Match Existing Technologies and Services to the Strategic Service Plan

The completed column A of Workform 3 provides the committee members with a comprehensive list of public services supported by technology. Now the committee members need to determine if these services are all worth continued support, or if one or more of them could be phased out. These decisions are best made in a meeting where committee members can discuss their discoveries and share their own knowledge and experiences as they relate to the library's current services.

Committee members should review each service listed on Workform 3 and identify which of the library's strategic objectives are being supported by that service. (See column B of figure 11.) If you can't find a direct link to the library's public service plan, ask yourselves if the service in question is an administrative function. If so, move it to

FIGURE 11

Workform 3, Strategic Plan Links—Example 2

A. Service	B. Strategic Plan Links or Admin/Staff	C. Sustain (S) Expand (E) Phase Out (P)
Adult Internet access— by reservation	Goal 2: Information Literacy Goal 3: General Information Goal 5: Formal Learning Support	
Adult Internet access— 15 minutes; no reservation	Goal 1: Current Topics and Titles Goal 3: General Information	
CD-ROM periodical databases	Goal 3: General Information Goal 5: Formal Learning Support	

Workform 4, Administrative Tools. Most library strategic plans focus on the delivery of customer services, and such plans rarely include discussions of the basic business technologies that any organization needs to operate in today's world. Obviously these business functions can have a technology component, and a thorough inventory will have included the devices being used to support these functions.

Step 3.3
Decide Which Existing Technologies and Services Should Be Sustained, Expanded, or Phased Out

ASSESSING WORKFORM 3, STRATEGIC PLAN LINKS

When you have finished matching the list of services on Workform 3 to the strategic plan, review the list of services again. Are there services on the list that are neither linked to the strategic plan nor identifiable as administrative functions or basic business services? If so, these are candidates to consider phasing out. The technologies being used to deliver these services might well be redeployed to deliver services that *are* a part of your strategic objectives or *will* support critical administrative functions. Even if the equipment being used can't be redeployed, you can certainly use the staff time spent on supporting these nonessential services in a more effective way.

After you have identified nonessential services, sort the data based on column B, putting the information on Workform 3 in the same priority order as the library's service goals, listing services linked to the most important goal at the top of the workform. Now review these services again. Compare the plan's objectives to the linked technologies. Ask yourself these questions:

> Is it the intent of the strategic plan to provide continuing support for the service at the current level, or does the plan call for expanding the service in question?

What measures of use are available for the committee to consider? Do the measures show stable usage or do they show a clear and continuing increase in demand?

What does the staff on the planning committee know empirically about the service in question? Does the service seem to be sufficiently meeting demand, or are there always customers waiting or being turned away because of limited resources?

If a single service objective is supported by more than one technology-based service, are all of those technologies still needed, or has one or more been superseded by the others?

Consider the answers to these questions. If the status quo seems to meet the needs and the technology-supported service being reviewed has not been superseded by other services supporting the same public service objective, then you have identified a service that needs to be sustained. The service supports a strategic objective and you need to continue to offer it. The resources you are expending on it seem sufficient, so continuing to offer the same level of service will produce the results identified in the objectives in the library's strategic plan. *This doesn't mean that you don't need to consider the service any further in your planning process.* Sustaining a technology-supported service requires regular investments to ensure that hardware and software are reliable and supportable. Technologies that are identified to be "sustained" will continue to be considered as the planning process proceeds.

If the strategic plan calls for expanding the service, or your own experience or staff comments indicate that demand exceeds capacity, then you have identified a service that should be considered for expansion. (See column C in figure 12 for an example.) Expanding a service doesn't always mean buying more; there are many ways to expand a service.

FIGURE 12
Workform 3, Strategic Plan Links—Example 3

A. Service	B. Strategic Plan Links or Admin/Staff	C. Sustain (S) Expand (E) Phase Out (P)
Adult Internet access— 15 minutes; no reservation	Goal 1: Current Topics and Titles Goal 3: General Information	S
Adult Internet access— by reservation	Goal 2: Information Literacy Goal 3: General Information Goal 5: Formal Learning Support	E
CD-ROM periodical databases	Goal 3: General Information Goal 5: Formal Learning Support	P

For example, many libraries simply do not have the physical space to house all of the PCs that the public might want to use. Adding a wireless "hot spot" in the library that enables customers to use their own Internet devices in the library (laptops, PDAs, cell phones, etc.) expands in-library access to electronic resources without adding more PCs. The combined creativity of the planning committee and the library's technology support staff can often identify ways to offer more access without physical expansion.

ASSESSING WORKFORM 4, ADMINISTRATIVE TOOLS

Deciding whether to recommend sustaining, expanding, or phasing out technology-supported administrative functions depends on the committee's empirical knowledge of the functions themselves or on information the committee members picked up during the inventory phase of the planning process. Do the functions supported seem to be provided in a timely manner, or is there always a backlog? If there is a backlog, is it attributable to lack of equipment or lack of staffing? Administrative systems such as finance or human resources may operate on separate networks or stand-alone workstations as security measures. This may result in limited access to the equipment or software itself, a problem that can be remedied through technology planning. If you identify such a system or service, the committee may recommend expanding the service. A technology that supports a basic administrative function without backlogs or delays will be sustained unless the committee knows that there is a plan to expand the service.

The members of the committee are unlikely to recommend phasing out an administrative service unless they discovered existing plans to do so during the inventory of services, or they uncovered two existing administrative services that seem to duplicate each other. Although it is not common to find duplicated administrative services, some organizations are so large that this problem can unknowingly develop. If your committee members think they have discovered such duplication, be sure to bring it to the attention of library administration.

REACHING AGREEMENT

As you can see, this part of the planning process requires that the committee members make a number of preliminary decisions. Sometimes it can be hard for a group of people to reach agreement, particularly if the topic is recommending the end of a service that your library currently offers. Appendix C, Groups Reaching Agreement, provides information on techniques the committee chair can use to bring committee members to consensus.[2]

When the members of the committee have finished reviewing and discussing Workform 3 and Workform 4, they will have completed the first phase of the planning process. They have prepared a list of the technology-supported public services and administrative functions that are currently being offered. They have identified which of these services and functions need to be sustained or expanded and which of them should be eliminated. The next task is to determine what new technology-supported services or administrative functions might be added.

TASK 4: IDENTIFY NEW SERVICES

In preparation for this task, committee members should review the library's public service goals and objectives, the list of current services that are supported by technology on Workform 3, and the current administrative functions that are supported by technology on Workform 4. The process of identifying opportunities for improving services or making staff functions more efficient or effective can be enjoyable if everyone remembers that there is no one right answer and that making suggestions for improvement doesn't mean the status quo is bad.

This part of the process is best done during a meeting of the committee where people can share their ideas and build on the suggestions of others. There are a number of ways a committee leader can stimulate the development and sharing of ideas in a group. Group discussions and brainstorming are two techniques commonly used in libraries. Nominal group technique and the Delphi Method are two other strategies for option development. The planning committee chair should read Appendix D, Groups Identifying Options, for discussions of how these techniques can be employed and some of the challenges groups can face as they try to develop options.

Regardless of which method is used, the purpose of this meeting of the committee is to identify additional ways in which technology can increase the likelihood that the library will achieve its objectives and to suggest technologies that will improve operating efficiency or effectiveness. No doubt during their research and conversations, one or more members of the committee will have found a number of "cool" technologies that would be fun to do, or unique to libraries, or even "the first time it has ever been done." While it is always fun to think about these types of things, stay focused on the fact that you are trying to improve the customer's ability to effectively use the services you want to offer and to run the library as efficiently as you can, not to play around on the cutting edge of technology. This doesn't mean you can't come up with some wonderfully creative ideas, but you need to pass those ideas through the reality check of relating them to the strategic plan or projecting what operational improvements they would actually yield.

Step 4.1
Identify Opportunities for More Effective Public Services through Technology Projects

Start by reviewing your goals and objectives. Are there goals and objectives that don't have any technology supporting them? Is that because no one can think of any technologies that would be useful? Be creative. Look at each public service goal. What will be required to reach it? If your strategic service plan was developed using *The New Planning for Results,* it includes measurable objectives that will result in achieving the goal. How might you use technology to achieve those objectives? Are there objectives that are supported by technology now but that may require more or different technology support to increase the chances of success?

As an example, a strategic plan might include the following goal and objectives:

Goal 2: Residents will have welcoming, vibrant, and dynamic places to meet and share with others.

Objective 1: During the next fiscal year, at least 600,000 Anytown residents will visit the library one or more times (ten per capita) and that number will increase by 3 percent each year.

Objective 2: During the next fiscal year, at least 300 bookings of meeting rooms will be made and that number will increase by 2 percent each year.

Could you encourage use of the meeting rooms by making it possible for groups to book rooms through the library's website, so they don't have to call when the business office is open? Could you add an e-commerce service permitting meeting room fees to be charged to credit cards, so they don't have to come in before their meeting to pay? How about encouraging visits by posting the complete schedule of library events open to the public on the website? Could you find a way to let groups booking the rooms for public events add their own entries to the online calendar so staff don't have to do it? What about developing and distributing a "What's Happening at the Library" newsletter based on the calendar, available either in print or as an e-mail attachment sent to people who sign up on your website to be notified about events?

When faced with the need to think about what additional technology-supported public services could be offered, committee members may throw up their hands and say "I don't even know where to start!" One obvious source of suggestions for new or improved services is the library staff. The members of the planning committee should be encouraged to talk with others on the staff about the public service goals and objectives and to gather the staff's thoughts about ways in which technology might assist them in achieving their part of the strategic goals.

Keeping up with technology trends is not solely the responsibility of members of the technology planning team or the technology support staff. Technology is so closely integrated with the basic services in most libraries that everyone uses it and every service is affected by it in one way or another. Everyone in your library who participates in the selection of materials or the design and delivery of public services should be responsible for keeping up with available technology products in his or her area of expertise. You expect the public service staff to bring a great new book or periodical title to a selector's attention if they hear of it; the same should be true for technology products.

Doing some research on what technology is available, or might be available in the near future, is another way to stimulate suggestions for consideration. Appendix A, Identifying Technology Options, suggests resources that can be used in researching options. The members of the technology planning committee were selected because they already have a basic knowledge of library technology or because they were interested and willing to learn. With the thorough grounding the committee members now have in what the library is already doing and their awareness of its strategic service objectives, their research efforts can focus on the areas relevant to your library's specific interests.

After taking the time to talk with staff or others who have some technology knowledge to share and doing some research on technologies that are available or projected to be available soon, the committee members will be able to share what they have learned and develop a list of recommendations for new projects that could be included in the library's technology plan.

Step 4.2
Identify Opportunities for More Efficient or Effective Administrative Functioning through Technology Projects

Remember that your technology plan can address administrative functions that would increase efficiency or make your staff more effective in delivering services as well as supporting direct public service. Many of the options in the meeting room example above would not only improve the customer's experience, but would also automate time-consuming staff activities.

Committee members should consider other ways to improve the efficiency of administrative functions. They can begin their discussions with the list of administrative functions that are currently supported by technology on Workform 4, Administrative Tools. Committee members talked to people who use those administrative tools while they were gathering the data for Workform 2. What kinds of concerns did those people express? What suggestions did they have? What did the committee members learn about new technologies that could improve administrative functions when they did their research? These questions should help stimulate a discussion that will identify possible enhancements to administrative functions.

Step 4.3
Evaluate Options

The committee's brainstorming has been very successful. The white board is full of great-sounding projects. Now what? How do you pick and choose among them? Start by sorting them out into one of three categories: public service support projects, administrative function projects, or both. You need to sort the projects into these categories because the criteria for evaluating technologies that support the delivery of public services are different from the criteria you apply to administrative functions that result in the reduction of backlogs or increased staff efficiency.

List the proposed public service support projects in column A of Workform 5, New Public Services Support Projects. (See figure 13.) List projects that will enhance administrative functions and projects that seem to support both administrative functions and public services on a new copy of Workform 4, Administrative Tools, that you label "New Projects."

FIGURE 13

Workform 5, New Public Services Support Projects—Example 1

A. Proposed Project	B. Strategic Plan/Objective	C. Relation to Target Audience	D. Relation to Intended Results	E. Appeal
E-commerce for booking meeting rooms				
Downloadable MP3 files for audiobooks				
Laptop lab for students				

1 = High   **2** = Moderate   **3** = Low

EVALUATING PUBLIC SERVICE TECHNOLOGIES

You will start by evaluating the services you listed in column A of Workform 5, New Public Services Support Projects. Evaluating your service support projects involves asking four questions:

> Which of our service objectives does this project support?
>
> Will the users of the technology be the intended audience of the service objective?
>
> Will the technology contribute directly to our service objective measures?
>
> Will the intended audience find the service interesting, beneficial, or fun?

As the group completes Workform 5, some of the ideas will fall away because, upon examination, they really can't be linked to the service plan. Others will make the service plan cut, but won't pass one of the other criteria. For example, if one of the objectives in your strategic plan is to increase the circulation of adult materials 5 percent next year, adding downloadable MP3 audiobook files to the collection may not help much if your audience primarily uses audiobooks during automobile-based commuting. As this book is being written, few cars include MP3 players and law enforcement discourages the use of headsets by vehicle drivers. It is likely that MP3 players will become a standard feature in cars over time, but try not to overestimate the speed with which a technology will be widely adopted. If you are too far ahead of the public's interest, you can spend a lot of time and money on a project whose time hasn't come. This highlights another benefit of technology planning as an ongoing process rather than a onetime event: you can monitor the growth in public interest and add a new project when you think the time is right. (See figure 14 for a completed example of Workform 5.)

When the members of the committee have completed Workform 5, they will have identified some public service projects that are worth considering for inclusion in the

FIGURE 14
Workform 5, New Public Services Support Projects—Example 2

A. Proposed Project	B. Strategic Plan/Objective	C. Relation to Target Audience	D. Relation to Intended Results	E. Appeal
E-commerce for booking meeting rooms	Goal 2: Commons	2	2	2
Downloadable MP3 files for audiobooks	Goal 1: Current Topics and Titles	3	3	3
Laptop lab for students	Goal 5: Formal Learning Support	1	1	1

1 = High   **2** = Moderate   **3** = Low

library's technology plan. These will be the technology-supported projects that link to one or more service objectives, that will be used by and appeal to the intended audience, and that will measurably contribute to achieving the library's goals and objectives.

EVALUATING ADMINISTRATIVE TECHNOLOGIES

When the members of the committee have completed their review of possible new technologies to support public service projects, they will move to a review of the suggestions that would enhance administrative functions. The criteria you use to evaluate technology-supported administrative functions include:

1. Identifying backlogs in operations that need to be resolved, and determining the benefit to the organization of relieving the backlogs
2. Projecting how much time you think the staff could save by introducing the proposed technology, then converting saved staff time to saved staff dollars, and comparing the projected cost savings to the costs of implementing the suggestion
3. Determining that a technology-supported administrative change would have a desirable public service impact that outweighs the fact that the cost exceeds the expected savings. An example of this type of change would be self-service checkout, the costs of which might not be justified by staff savings, but which would give the customer the benefits of shorter lines and greater customer privacy. Another example might be accepting credit card payments for fines and fees through the online catalog. Although it probably wouldn't save measurable amounts of staff time at the circulation desk, it could well result in more people paying and it would definitely make it easier or more convenient for them to do so.

When you review the new projects on the copy of Workform 4, Administrative Tools, that you labeled "New Projects," you will find that some of the possible new projects address operational backlogs. Whenever confronted with an operational backlog, the committee's empirical knowledge of the current problem and the benefit to the organization of resolving it is the basis of your decision making. How many people does the backlog affect? Is it a minor irritant or a major barrier to getting the job done? Will a small amount of investment (e.g., adding another PC) resolve it, or does it require a complete rethinking of the installed technology (e.g., scrapping the current accounting system and selecting and installing a new one)? If a small investment will measurably improve the situation, acknowledge that and add the project to the list. If you need a major investment, then you should evaluate the project as you would a new efficiency project.

When evaluating efficiency projects, even those that fall into the third type of project listed above, you will need to compare the costs of the project to the dollars you will save. The amount of time it will take you to recover the cost of implementing the technology is the "payback period." Once you've reached the payback point, the savings accrue to the library. With technologies, the payback period generally should be less than the anticipated life of the technology. If you make a decision to purchase a technology so expensive relative to its savings that it doesn't have a realistic payback period, you need to know that, too.

When the committee is considering options designed to increase staff efficiency, it is not expected to do detailed cost-benefit analyses, just general projections of potential savings. These projections can then be used later on in the planning process when the costs of implementing suggested technologies are developed.

Workform 6, Evaluating Efficiency Projects: Staff Savings, will help you develop savings projections. To complete this workform, committee members will gather the information needed to be able to project the possible time savings. This will require committee members to talk with the staff currently involved in the process under consideration. For example, one suggested project might be to add a web interface to the payroll system so staff can complete their weekly time sheets electronically. In researching this, a planning committee member discovers that there are three people involved in time sheets: the staff member who completes the form, his or her supervisor who approves it, and the business office staff who key the information into the payroll system. The staff member's time is unchanged because it doesn't take appreciably less time to key in hours than it does to write them. The supervisor's time is unchanged, since she still has to review and approve the electronic entry. But the business office staff time is completely eliminated. The business office staffer says she can enter about fifteen time cards an hour and the library has sixty staff to pay each week. After completing Workform 6 (see figure 15), cost projections show an annual $2,600 savings in staff time. If later in the planning process, you determine that licensing the web interface for the payroll system costs $500 and implementation will require one day of your webmaster's time to install, configure, and test, then the payback period for this project could be less than half a year.

When Workform 6 is completed for each proposed project that would enhance administrative functions, the committee should review all of them to select projects for inclusion in the plan. In reviewing the workforms, you may find that some projected savings are so small that it hardly seems worth doing. Other projects offer significant savings potential. You may also find that some suggestions don't represent large savings, but the staff time involved is desperately needed for other projects and freeing it up is worth the investment. These are the projects the committee will want to consider for inclusion in the technology plan, along with any you judge to have the potential to significantly improve the customers' experience of library services.

FIGURE 15
Example of Workform 6, Evaluating Efficiency Projects: Staff Savings

---

Project: ___Self-entered time sheets/Web interface___

Job classification: ___All staff___

A. Anticipated savings in time per transaction | 0

B. Number of times each transaction is completed annually | _____

C. Total anticipated time saved (minutes) | _____

D. Total anticipated time saved (hours) | _____

E. Average personnel cost per hour | _____

F. Anticipated annual personnel cost savings | _____

Job classification: ___Supervisors___

A. Anticipated savings in time per transaction | 0

B. Number of times each transaction is completed annually | _____

C. Total anticipated time saved (minutes) | _____

D. Total anticipated time saved (hours) | _____

E. Average personnel cost per hour | _____

F. Anticipated annual personnel cost savings | _____

Job classification: ___Business office staff___

A. Anticipated savings in time per transaction | 4 minutes

B. Number of times each transaction is completed annually | 3,120

C. Total anticipated time saved (minutes) | 12,480

D. Total anticipated time saved (hours) | 208

E. Average personnel cost per hour | $12.50

F. Anticipated annual personnel cost savings | $2,600.00

SUMMARY

G. Total anticipated time saved (hours) | 208

H. Total anticipated annual personnel cost savings | $2,600.00

Step 4.4
Create a List of Technology Projects to Sustain, Expand, Phase Out, and Add

When the committee has completed evaluating the potential new projects on Workform 5 and Workform 6, it is ready to create a list of the technology projects it thinks should be included in the technology plan. This list will include the committee members' preliminary recommendations on which existing public or administrative services technologies should be sustained, which should be expanded, and which should be phased out (Workform 3 and Workform 4). The list will also include the committee's suggested new technology projects (Workform 5 and Workform 6).

Step 4.5
Make a Preliminary Presentation to the Library Administration

At this stage it is a good idea for the technology planning committee to make a presentation of its work to date to the library's administrative staff. The next tasks in the planning process will be based on the list of projects to be sustained, expanded, added, or phased out. Before you proceed to further work on the list, you will want to determine if the library's senior managers agree with the preliminary recommendations.

Prepare for the presentation by creating a document consisting of two parts. The first part will list the library's service goals in priority order. Under each service goal, write the current technology-based public services the committee is recommending be sustained. Next list the existing services related to this service goal that the committee recommends be expanded. For each expansion project, include a brief explanation of why the committee is recommending expansion. The third section under each service goal is a list of the new projects the committee is recommending, with a link to the specific measurable objective the new project supports. Finally, list the existing technology-based services that you are recommending be phased out, with a brief explanation of why that recommendation is made.

The second part of the document lists administrative functions in the same order: technologies to be sustained; technologies to be expanded, with a brief explanation of why expansion is recommended; new technologies to consider, with an estimate of the expected staff time savings or an explanation of why the technology should be adopted without any clear savings justification; and technologies to be phased out, with an explanation of why the committee believes they are no longer needed. (See figure 16 for an example of this document.)

FIGURE 16
Example of Preliminary Presentation to Administrative Staff

Service Goals	Administrative Functions
SERVICE GOAL 1: *Current Topics and Titles*	*Current Technologies to Be Sustained*
Current Technologies to Be Sustained	Replace the e-mail server hardware
Adult Internet access—15-minute limit	Existing equipment out of warranty and increas-
Occasional backlogs of users not frequent or	ingly unstable; unable to support current release
long enough to warrant additional investments	of e-mail server software
Current Technologies to Be Expanded	Establish a virtual private network for library finance
None	staff to connect with the commercial payroll service
New Technologies to Be Added	Payroll vendor upgrading technology and paper
None	payroll reports will no longer be accepted
Current Technologies to Be Phased Out	
None	*Current Technologies to Be Expanded*
	None
SERVICE GOAL 3: *Information Literacy*	
Current Technologies to Be Sustained	*New Technologies to Be Added*
Adult Internet access—15-minute limit	Add a spam filter to the library's network
See Goal 1	Increasing spam in e-mail taxes library band-
Current Technologies to Be Expanded	width and wastes staff time in managing, reading,
Adult Internet access—by reservation	and responding to e-mail; spam also increases
All available time slots frequently booked	likelihood of introducing viruses into the network
before midday at main library and Elm branch;	Install Help Desk management software
recommend adding PCs in both locations	Web interface to permit public services and
New Technologies to Be Added	support services staff to report problems online
Digital projector for Ash branch computer lab	and view status of calls; statistics on types and
Increased attendance at computer lab classes	duration of calls and mean response times will
on using digital resources can be supported	track IT performance and identify the types of
with a large-screen display capability, reducing	skills needed on IT staff.
the number of turnaways	
Current Technologies to Be Phased Out	
None	
SERVICE GOAL 4: *General Information*	
Current Technologies to Be Sustained	
Adult Internet access—15-minute limit	
See Goal 1	
Current Technologies to Be Expanded	
Adult Internet access—by reservation	
See Goal 3	
New Technologies to Be Added	
None	
Current Technologies to Be Phased Out	
CD-ROM periodical databases	
Superceded by Internet e-resources; no longer	
needed	

The committee chair can use this document as a handout in the presentation. The outcome of the presentation should be a list of technologies that the administrative staff agrees should be explored and would be willing to consider implementing, if available funding and staffing permit.

Part 2 of the Tree County Public Library case study illustrates that portion of the planning process discussed in this chapter.

PART 2

Evaluating Existing Services

The members of the technology planning committee have been busy gathering a great deal of data. They have worked from the inventory provided by the IT department and completed their visits to each library branch and department. Using what they learned, they have completed Workform 2. The committee chair has merged the data from column D on all of the copies of Workform 2 and recorded that data in column A of Workform 3 or Workform 4 as appropriate. Copies of the library's strategic plan and the last two years of usage statistics are sent out along with copies of Workforms 3 and 4 in preparation for the meeting.

The chair has scheduled the meeting with two agenda items: to review the current technology-supported services and functions, and to discuss possible new projects. In the first part of the meeting, the members discuss each service on Workform 3 and each function on Workform 4. They agree on a couple of public services that can be phased out. Each library branch has one Windows 3.1 machine with early versions of word-processing and spreadsheet software "because the computers still work and some customers may still have those programs at home." Each branch also still has a couple of CD-ROM periodical databases in a networked CD tower "in case the Internet connection goes down." Committee members decide to recommend phasing out the Windows 3.1 machines and the CD-ROM periodical databases.

The committee decides to recommend sustaining all of the technology-based administrative functions and the remaining public services, except for a lively debate on the number of PC workstations that should be set up as OPAC-only stations. Everyone finally agrees that a single workstation in each branch and one in each main library department will be enough. The committee will recommend that the remaining OPAC-only PCs be turned into general-use PCs with Internet access.

What's Next?

In an organization large enough to have a dedicated technology support staff, the next task, an assessment of your current technological infrastructure, will typically be done by that staff. If you don't have a dedicated technology staff, or if all of the technology support staff are members of the committee, then the next task will be shared among committee members. The committee will also be responsible for the task of assessing the technology skills of the staff and determining what additional skills are needed.

NOTES

1. A server is a "computer or device on a network that manages network resources. For example, a file server is a computer and storage device dedicated to storing files. Any user on the network can store files on the server" (*Webopedia,* http://www.webopedia.com/TERM/s/server.html).
2. Appendix C, Groups Reaching Agreement, is reprinted from Nelson, *The New Planning for Results,* 235–45.

Chapter 3

Assess

MILESTONES

By the time you finish this chapter you will know how to

- identify the new or upgraded technology resources (hardware, software, networks) needed to support the possible services and projects
- identify the staff skills needed to support the possible services and projects
- assess the technical skill levels of your staff
- develop estimates of costs and staff time needed to implement those projects

The work the technology planning committee has done to this point has focused on identifying the *technology-related services and functions* your library currently offers or wants to add. Now it is time to consider what *tools* you have and what *tools* you will need to make those services or functions happen. To do this you will complete an assessment of the current technical infrastructure (hardware, software, and networks) in your library. This assessment is different than the inventory of equipment you worked with earlier; it goes beyond the list of what you own now by including information on upgrades you have already committed to and technical developments that staff may already be monitoring. After you have identified your technical starting point, you will look at your list of recommended technology-supported projects to determine the technological infrastructure they will require. Finally, you will consider the technology requirements for the recommended projects and decide how difficult and costly it will be to implement each of them.

Sustaining Current Services

One important result of technology planning should be to ensure that you have the necessary resources to sustain your current successful programs. You do this by understanding what technologies you have in place today and what investments you may need to make to keep those programs operating in the future.

TASK 5: ASSESS THE CURRENT TECHNOLOGY ENVIRONMENT

Step 5.1
Assess Future Upgrades or Replacement Requirements for Existing Infrastructure to Sustain Services

The technical inventory you have of the library's infrastructure describes the baseline from which your technology planning can proceed. The first question you need to ask about that baseline infrastructure is, "What pieces of this need to be upgraded or replaced during the term of the plan we are developing?" Your focus at this point is on upgrades or replacements that are needed so you can sustain the services you are already offering. You will look at what will be required to expand or add services later.

Why might you need to consider upgrading or replacing software or hardware if the services that are being supported by that technology are already in place? One reason might be that the software you are using is so old that you can no longer get support for it. Most software developers offer new releases of their software on a regular basis. This is true for both the applications you run (word processing, web browsers, spreadsheets, etc.) and for computer operating systems (software that performs basic tasks such as recognizing input from the keyboard, sending output to the display screen, keeping track of files on the disk, and controlling peripheral devices such as disk drives and printers). As the new releases of software arrive, support for the older versions is often phased out. This means that if you want support for your software, you need to be within at least one or two releases of the most current version of that software. A new release of software often requires more computing capacity from the hardware it runs on. This can lead to the need to upgrade or replace hardware in order to stay current with the software.

Another reason you might need to replace hardware is because it is worn out. This is particularly true of hardware used by the public. If your technology support staff keeps records on the frequency of repairs for the library's equipment (and they should), then reviewing the repair records is a good way to identify equipment that is ready to be replaced. Of course, most staff can easily identify for you the equipment in their area that hinders rather than helps them in the performance of their jobs. If you don't have repair records, ask the staff who work with the equipment every day which pieces need to be replaced. You could also ask the vendors of major technological resources (such as your integrated library system) if there is a phaseout schedule for the support of their hardware or software.

As noted in the previous chapter, this part of the assessment process could be completed by the technology support staff in the library—if the library has a technology support staff. In smaller libraries, the members of the technology planning committee will probably be responsible for this part of the process, as they were for the earlier parts of it. By this point, the members of the committee are probably better informed about the library's infrastructure than anyone else on the staff.

Workform 7, Infrastructure Assessment, provides a form on which to record the data about your current infrastructure and to record the needed upgrades or replacements you identify. Start by combining the individual pieces of equipment in your inventory into logical groups and complete a copy of Workform 7 for each group of technology. (If your current inventory of technology is organized by branches, you may need to add the branches' equipment together by type to complete Workform 7.) Some groupings you might want to consider are

- staff workstations and peripherals
- public workstations and peripherals
- servers
- network equipment and circuits or bandwidth
- server software
- staff software applications
- public software applications, with separate groups for children and adults if you have separate sets of software for each

Depending on your own local environment, there may be a few other groups you need as well, e.g., adaptive technologies. (See figure 17 for a completed example of Workform 7.)

Summarize your technical inventory for each group in section 2 (Baseline Technology) of Workform 7. Use section 3 (Retirement Targets) to list any hardware or software in the group that supports services the planning committee is recommending for phaseout. Sections 5 (Existing Commitments and Needed Upgrades) and 8 (Future Possibilities) provide a place to record equipment or software upgrades needed to support current services, short term and long term. Section 5 also includes a place to record any planned upgrades the library has already committed to make but has not yet done.

Step 5.2
Assess Staff Skills

The staff's technical skills are crucial to successfully implementing a technology plan. The best and most relevant technology that money can buy will never fully deliver on its promise if the staff can't use it well. Assessing the technical skills your staff have now will help in identifying the future training needs that may result from your technology plan.

FIGURE 17

Example of Workform 7, Infrastructure Assessment

1. Technology: ___Desktop Hardware and Operating Systems—Public___

CURRENT	WITHIN 12–18 MONTHS	2–3 YEARS
2. Baseline Technology Pentium, 133MHz, 64MB, WIN 98, 10GB HD (5) Celeron, 300 MHz, 128MB, WIN 2000, 20GB HD (15) Pentium III, 1.3 GHz, 512MB, 30GB HD, WIN XP (30) HP flatbed scanner (1)	**5. Existing Commitments and Needed Upgrades** Add 5 new PCs to Adult Reference area—main library (committed) Replace Pentium 133 MHz (5)	**8. Future Possibilities** Add 2 more PCs in Children's area of each branch (14 total)—expand Upgrade Celeron Win 2000 to XP—sustain
3. Retirement Targets	**6. Developments to Monitor**	
4. Support Only Celeron, 300 MHz, 128MB, 20GB HD (15) Pentium III, 1.3 GHz, 512MB, 30GB IID, WIN XP (30)	**7. Issues and Dependencies** Celerons meet minimum recommended requirements for WIN XP; test possible upgrade before committing to upgrade to XP	

WHAT INFORMATION DO YOU NEED?

The level of technical expertise that a library staff needs is directly related to the variety and complexity of the library's technologies. While the levels of technical skill required to operate and manage a library's technology vary from library to library, there are two sets of skills that every library needs on staff: staff who know how to use the available technologies and staff who know how to manage those technologies. All staff need to be able to effectively use the resources you have installed which are related to the jobs they are expected to perform. The library technology support staff, whether it is an entire department or a single person who supports your PCs on an as-needed basis, may need additional skills.

Workform 8, Technical Skills Assessment, contains a list of basic technical skills that any library staff member needs to function effectively in a library today. Workform 8 also includes a list of basic skills recommended for technical support staff. You can use this workform as a starting point for developing your own form to inventory your staff's level of comfort with technology. (See figure 18.)

FIGURE 18
Example of Workform 8, Technical Skills Assessment

PART 1: Basic Technology Skills

Software	No Skill		Some Ability		Proficient
Create, format, save, print, and open a document using word processing	O	O	O	O	O
Send, receive, read, and respond to e-mail messages	O	O	O	O	O
Attach files to e-mail and read files received as attachments	O	O	O	O	O

The list of skills on Workform 8 is by no means exhaustive. There are probably other skills that staff members need to have in order to do their jobs. For example, there are likely to be skills associated with your online catalog or circulation system that staff must have, such as the ability to do a complex search of titles in the OPAC or to register customers or pay fines in the integrated system.

Some libraries and library systems have developed lists of technological competencies for their staff and share these through their websites. You may want to look at these sites for additional suggestions. The Oakland Public Library in California developed a list of its minimum technology competencies for all job classifications and work locations in the library as a first step in developing a technology training program for library staff. The Rochester Regional Library Council, a multitype library network serving libraries and library systems in the five-county Rochester region of New York, offers its members checklists of basic competencies in a variety of areas (for example, basic hardware, file management, and e-mail).[1] The council also offers links to resources for self-help in developing needed skills.

Although developing a list of core technological competencies is not a requirement for developing a technology plan, it is an activity your library may want to undertake. Core competencies are the minimum skills any staff member needs to be effective in completing his or her job. The core competencies you identify should be included in every library job description and used as a basis for making hiring decisions. Core competencies can also be used as guidelines for setting training objectives in annual personnel evaluations. A list of expected core competencies and a survey of the current state of staff skills can be used together to develop a librarywide training program to ensure that all staff have the skills they need to be successful in their jobs.

WHERE CAN YOU GET THE INFORMATION?

The easiest way to assess your staff's comfort and skill level with technology is to ask them. However, you need to be sure that the staff understand that this assessment of their skills is simply intended to identify training needs. You want to be sure that the process doesn't make the staff feel "stupid" or inadequate. Technology is changing so fast that most staff feel inadequate with at least some of the library's hardware and software.

Workform 8, Technical Skills Assessment, or a similar form you develop specifically for your own library's requirements, can be used to gather this information from the staff. Provide each staff member with a copy of the workform and ask them to complete it and return it to a member of the planning committee. When the forms are returned, one or two members of the committee can compile the results and report to the group on the percentage of staff who judge themselves to be proficient, somewhat skilled, or untrained in the various skills you have defined.

If you have staff who possess the skills to design databases using tools like Microsoft's Access or Excel programs, you can develop a database or spreadsheet with a form-based user interface that you can put on the library's internal website. As staff complete the form online, they will be creating a database for the committee to review.

If you don't have the skills or the time to build your own electronic data-collection tool, TechSurveyor offers a basic staff skill survey that staff can receive via e-mail and complete online.[2] TechSurveyor will compile the results for you and report on staff who may need training in the surveyed areas and on staff who could act as technology mentors.

Step 5.3
Develop Cost Estimates for Upgrades or Replacements Needed to Sustain Current Services

You listed the hardware, software, and network equipment or bandwidth upgrades you may need to invest in just to sustain current services in sections 5 and 8 of Workform 7, Infrastructure Assessment. The next step is to develop cost estimates for these investments.

WHAT INFORMATION DO YOU NEED?

The cost of new technology involves more than just the initial purchase price. It may also include the cost of installing the equipment, the cost of any needed software, and perhaps an annual maintenance fee or the purchase of an extended warranty.

Remember, too, that just because your staff is doing the installation doesn't mean the installation is free. Staff time costs money, too. Your technology support staff probably has enough experience with the technologies that need to be upgraded or replaced to give you a reasonable estimate of the time required, and you can calculate the cost of installation by multiplying the time required by the cost per hour. If there are no library staff members with the required skills, ask the vendor to give an estimate of the cost of installation.

Use Workform 9, Costs to Sustain Services, to calculate the estimated costs of each of the upgrades and replacements you have identified. (See figure 19.)

WHERE CAN YOU GET THE INFORMATION?

You can obtain quotations for purchase prices from a variety of sources, depending on the type of hardware or software you are trying to buy. Peripherals, desktop workstations,

FIGURE 19

Example of Workform 9, Costs to Sustain Services

1. Equipment, software, or bandwidth to be purchased: _PCs for P133 replacement_

EQUIPMENT/SOFTWARE		
2. Number of items to be purchased	5	
3. Cost per item	$1,500	
4. Total cost of items to be purchased		$7,500
WARRANTY/MAINTENANCE		
5. Cost of warranty per item	3 yr incl.	
6. Annual maintenance cost per item	n/a	
7. Total cost of warranty or annual maintenance		$0

and most local area network equipment can be purchased from local computer stores, from Internet sources, or from state or local government contracts. If your library is part of a larger governmental unit, there may be local procurement regulations you need to follow in getting quotes for new hardware or software. For the purposes of this step in the technology planning process, you just need a reasonable estimate of what the hardware or software will cost through whichever procurement process you will be using, not the rock-bottom lowest price you can find. The costs you are developing will be used for budget planning purposes, and you don't want to shortchange your plan by budgeting too little.

If you are estimating the costs of expanding the bandwidth of your wide area network (WAN), you will need to talk with your telecommunications circuit provider. This could be the local phone company, a cable television supplier, the staff at your consortium headquarters, or a local or state government agency. Your technology support staff should know who to contact for cost estimates. WAN equipment cost estimates may be available through your bandwidth supplier, your integrated library system supplier, or from vendors that specialize in designing and providing equipment for wide area networks.

SUMMARIZING THE COSTS

After completing all of the Workform 9s for the upgrades and replacements you need to sustain the current level of technology-based services, add them all together. You now have a reasonable estimate of what it will cost to support your current level of technology-based services over the next several years. The planning committee is ready to move on to assessing the requirements of new or expanded services.

Assessing New or Expanded Services

Turn your attention back to the list approved by the administration in Step 4.5. This list includes both the current services that the committee thinks might need to be expanded and the new services the committee is considering recommending. These entries on the list are the basis for the next task.

TASK 6: DETERMINE THE REQUIREMENTS OF NEW OR EXPANDED SERVICES

Task 1: Identify Results

Task 2: Choose the Committee

Task 3: Evaluate Existing Services

Task 4: Identify New Services

Task 5: Assess the Current Technology Environment

Task 6: Determine the Requirements of New or Expanded Services

    Step 6.1: Determine technical infrastructure, skills requirements, and costs for expanded or new services.

    Step 6.2: Identify available staff resources with the necessary skills.

    Step 6.3: Develop time estimates for each project or pilot as needed.

Task 7: Select and Present

Task 8: Inform

Task 9: Implement the Projects in the Plan

Task 10: Sustain the Planning Process

Expanding services or adding new services probably means you will be investing in additional technology to support those services. It may also mean that additional staff skills will be required to implement or use the new services. All of these options will have costs associated with them. This series of steps helps you identify these costs and needed skills so that you can factor this data into your final selection of technologies to recommend for inclusion in the plan.

Step 6.1
Determine Technical Infrastructure, Skills Requirements, and Costs for Expanded or New Services

When you investigated the options in Task 4, Identify New Services, you probably identified one or more suppliers for many of the technologies the committee was considering. Now it is time to talk with those suppliers to get an understanding of the technical requirements to support their products. If the library has a dedicated technology support staff, this step will typically be done by that staff. Otherwise, the members of the planning committee will be responsible for this step.

WHAT DO YOU NEED TO KNOW?

New Services

The questions you need to ask potential suppliers of the technology required to support your new services are:

> What hardware (servers, desktop workstations, peripherals), software, and network configuration are needed to support your product?
>
> What are the bandwidth requirements of the product?
>
> Do you supply the hardware and the software? Does the library need to deal with any third parties for any portion of the equipment or

software? Does the library have the option to purchase any of the hardware or software from another supplier or to use currently installed equipment? If so, which pieces?

If the library's requirements grow, are there increased costs for more users or more sites?

What skills will our staff need to support your product on an ongoing basis? What level of operational support is typically required?

What skills are needed to install and configure your product? Will you provide those services? At what cost?

What type of ongoing service and support do you offer for the product? At what cost?

What training do you offer on the product?

When you contact a potential supplier, you should be prepared to provide the vendor with the following information:

the number of sites expected to use the product

the number of simultaneous users expected to use the product

a brief overview of your current technology environment, including your standard workstation and server operating systems (Windows, Macintosh, or Linux)

Fortunately, your planning process to this point has given you ready answers to these questions.

Be very clear about the requirements you may have for interfacing any planned new equipment or services with the software or hardware you already have. For example, if you are considering a service that you will offer only to registered borrowers, then that technology needs to interface with your integrated library system. Most integrated library system (ILS) vendors will permit third-party systems to validate users against the customer database, but they expect the supplier of the third-party product to do the work necessary to make it happen. If your staff thinks they can buy the hardware and software and install it themselves, be sure *they* know how to do the interfacing required and that doing it yourselves will not adversely affect your warranties or maintenance agreements.

Underestimate rather than overestimate your staff's abilities to install and configure new technologies. Staff time costs money, too. If the project represents a new challenge for your staff, you need to allow for the learning curve costs. Often it is best to hire the supplier to install the first phase of your new project and ensure that your staff members work with the supplier to learn what is being done. Then, in subsequent phases, you will have the expertise available on your staff to do the work in-house, if you choose.

EXPANDED SERVICES

If you are investigating the technology required to expand current services, you will want to ask potential suppliers of that technology some of the same questions. You need to know the following:

What hardware (servers, desktop workstations, peripherals), software, and network configuration are needed to expand the use of this product?

Will expanding the service have an impact on our network bandwidth? If so, what?

Does the vendor supply the hardware and the software? Does the library need to deal with any third parties for any portion of the equipment or software? Can we deal with third parties if we choose to do so? Can we use any currently installed hardware or software?

Will the vendor provide installation and testing services? At what cost?

What will be the cost for service and support on the expanded product?

Be prepared to provide the potential supplier with the same information on expected use and current environment.

If your staff have experience with the technology you are buying, then you may already know approximately how long it will take staff to install, test, and configure the new hardware and software. For example, if you are adding a new server and fifteen new PCs to an existing network that was installed by library technology staff, you can check with the staff who installed the original network and get a fairly accurate estimate of the installation costs. You can compare the cost of doing the work in-house to the cost quotes for those services from your potential suppliers and decide which option makes the best financial sense. If the original network was installed by a vendor, you can check the invoices to see what the costs were at that time. This will give you a general idea of the costs you can expect for installation now.

It is likely that you will have multiple people speaking with multiple vendors to gather the information listed above. It will ease review of the data collected, and increase the chances that all the necessary data will be gathered, if you provide staff with forms to complete as they are working with the vendors. Workform 10, Requirements of New or Expanded Services, is an example of the type of form you can use during the data collection process. (See figure 20.)

FIGURE 20
Example of Workform 10, Requirements of New or Expanded Services

1. Project Name: _Digital projector for Ash branch computer lab_

2. Vendor/Product: _Infocus LP 640_

3. List hardware, software, and network requirements. Include all purchase costs.
Hardware and cables only—projector and DVI cables for connecting to PC
Projector—$1,999.00
Cables—$80.00

4. List bandwidth requirements, if any.
None

WHERE CAN YOU GET THE INFORMATION?

Often the hardware, software, and network equipment you think you may want to add can be purchased from a variety of sources. Pricing for these items will range from the manufacturer's suggested retail price offered by full-service vendors to deeply discounted prices offered from mail-order or web sources and technology superstores. The purchase options for technology are very similar to shopping in department stores. If you want a personal shopper to help you pick out the perfect item, you go to Macy's, Dillard's, or Nordstrom and expect to pay retail prices. The store will arrange to have the item tailored, if need be, and will take a return, no questions asked, if you bring the item back a month later. But if you know what you want, don't mind waiting in line, and are willing to have the item altered yourself, there are plenty of other stores that will sell you the same product at reduced prices. Just remember, you are expected to serve yourself—personal attention doesn't come with the reduced prices.

This same spectrum ranging from full-service/retail pricing to self-reliance/discount pricing exists in the world of technology. There are full-service suppliers that will analyze your functional requirements and present you with a proposal for the hardware, software, training, installation, and maintenance of a range of technology products. They will take a request such as "We want a self-service computer reservation system that uses the customer's library card to register for PC time, includes the ability to sign up for a guest card, and charges for printing" and design the system you need. These suppliers will give you proposals for all the equipment and software necessary. Their services will even include providing you with site preparation information on the data cabling and electrical service you will need to support the new service. Although you will need to know enough about the technology you are trying to install to be able to understand the components of the vendor's proposal, or at least enough to ask intelligent questions and understand the answers, working with a full-service supplier lets you "outsource" the design of the system, the identification of an appropriate set of hardware and software components, and the installation and testing of the products.

Full-service suppliers include many of the traditional library automation vendors and local or national technology supply firms. The advantage of using the traditional library vendors as full-service suppliers is their knowledge of the operational environment of public libraries. They usually understand that much of the technology they are being asked to quote will be used by the general public and that security of the client devices and ease of use are paramount. General technology suppliers are more experienced with business applications and more oriented toward designing solutions to be used only by staff. Their assumptions about security needs may revolve around keeping users from accessing specific network resources, not keeping them from accessing the client machine's operating system. A library that wants to work with a local firm that has had little or no public access experience needs to be very explicit about the operating environment it expects to support. Sometimes a library consultant can help facilitate communication between the library staff and a local supplier that doesn't understand the library's environment.

If you have the technical expertise on staff to design and support your own networks and to identify the components you want to buy, you can create a list of the desired equipment and services and solicit price quotes from various potential suppliers. The degree of support you require in the installation, configuration, and testing of the equipment and software will determine which firms will give you quotes. Be sure to think through carefully the services you will need and be very explicit about them in your conversations with potential suppliers or in whatever documents you produce to solicit quotes.

Step 6.2
Identify Available Staff Resources
with the Necessary Skills

Your investigation of the options in Step 6.1 identified the skills needed to install and support the products under consideration. Now you need to determine if your technology support staff have those skills.

Create a list of the necessary skills identified in your conversations with potential suppliers using Workform 11, Technical Skills Needed. These might be such things as "ability to load software on PCs," "ability to add a server to the network," or "experience with SQL." Next to each identified technical skill, write the name of the staff member or members who have that skill. If no member of your staff has the necessary skill, leave the name field blank. (See figure 21.)

FIGURE 21
Example of Workform 11, Technical Skills Needed

Project Name: _____ Pentium 133 replacements _____

Vendor: _____ Gateway _____

REQUIRED SKILLS	STAFF MEMBER
Unpack and assemble hardware	John
Configure and test PC operating systems and software	Ruth

PROJECTS TAKE TIME

Be realistic about the staffing requirements of your ever-expanding technology infrastructure. You can't keep adding projects and technologies without adding the staff time needed to support them. Your technical services department can't handle a bigger materials budget each year without more staff, increased outsourcing, or backlogs. Your technology support staff operates under exactly the same conditions. They will need increased resources to cope with an increased workload—or you will be facing backlogs there too.

As part of the planning process, the technology support staff need to estimate how many staff hours are available to spend on projects. All technology departments split their time between maintenance functions (keeping what you've already got running) and new projects. You need to determine the amount of staff time spent on maintenance before you can know what staff resources are available for new projects. If your library has been using a help desk software package such as Remedy, Track It, or Help Star, information about the time spent on maintenance should be readily at hand. Some libraries have staff specifically dedicated to maintenance and other staff specifically charged with project management and new system implementation. If your library doesn't have good data on maintenance time requirements, ask the technology support staff to estimate these for now. Then encourage them to begin tracking the information so in the future you can work with better data than just a guesstimate.

If your IT department manager or your IT staff member reports that there is absolutely no time available to consider doing anything new, the committee chair will want to suggest a review of the department or person's current work tasks to see if there are tasks being done that could be phased out or handled by other staff. This review process should be done by the IT person's supervisor, not the technology planning committee. But the technology committee chair should request a report on the results of the review.

Even after you get the data or the estimate, remember that the average 40-hour employee, who is paid for 2,080 hours per year, actually only works about 1,728 hours per year.[3] A technology support group of six has a theoretical maximum of about 10,368 available hours annually. Of course, not all of these can be assigned to project work. There are also "nonproductive" hours taken up by other activities such as meetings, training, staff reviews, etc. There are external issues that need to be taken into consideration as well. If the library is building a new facility, technology staff may well have additional duties. The time of year will also affect the amount of time available for new or expanded projects. The period between Thanksgiving and the first of the year is normally so full of holiday activities that it can be very difficult for staff to keep up with their routine responsibilities, let alone take on new tasks. Subtracting the time spent on maintenance and the nonproductive time from the theoretical maximum results in the hours available to be allocated to projects. A six-person department could easily have only 5,000 project hours available.

Fortunately, just as you can outsource some of your technical and administrative services, you can also outsource some of your technology support activities. Simply buying extended warranties on all your desktop workstations instead of expecting your own staff to fix every broken PC can help a great deal. It is a good idea to replace workstations, especially public workstations, when they are no longer covered by a warranty. You can contract with an outside service to do training and support on office automation packages. Consider hiring a vendor to manage all the public printers in your buildings, the same way you hire someone to manage your photocopiers. If you discover that there really isn't any time available in your technology support group to implement the new projects you are considering, you might want to go back to Step 4.1 and discuss ways that the technology support group can be more efficient in some of the tasks they do now. Then include some of those suggestions in your technology plan.

Step 6.3
Develop Time Estimates for Each Project or Pilot as Needed

In this step you will project the amount of staff time that will be required for each potential project. Workform 12, Project Time Estimates, will help you gather and organize this information. *Remember that you identified projects needed to sustain current services in Step 5. You also need to include these projects in the time estimates you develop.*

There are five stages in the life of any technology project:

Needs assessment is the phase of the project in which the functional and technical requirements are defined. This is a more detailed definition of the project requirements than the planning process you are in now. Think of this as developing the specifications. Needs assessment defines criteria that can be used to select from multiple suppliers of appropriate products.

Selection is the formal process of acquiring the product and services. Typical activities include issuing Requests for Proposals or Request for Quotes, participating in functional demonstrations, interviewing current users of the product, and completing purchasing processes.

Implementation typically includes hardware and software installation, configuration, testing, and training.

Maintenance describes the period of ongoing use and support of the product or service. Activities include system administration, user support, software upgrades, and enhancement.

Retirement is the purposeful decommissioning of a product or service and its removal from the library. This happens when the migration to a replacement system is completed or when a product that is no longer needed is deinstalled.

In order to estimate the time needed for a project, you will have to determine how much time will be required to get to the maintenance stage and how many additional staff hours will be required to maintain the project. Some but not all projects include a retirement stage, and you will need to estimate the amount of time it will take to replace older equipment, migrate to a new integrated library system, decommission a population of older PCs, etc.

A completed Workform 12 is shown in figure 22. Note that the times estimated in the figure are actual work hours, not the total elapsed time the project will take. There will be waiting periods between the steps listed above—for example, between placing the order and receiving, unboxing, and setting up the PCs—that will extend the total elapsed time well beyond the 5¾ days listed in the example.

How do you know how much time will be needed for a project? One way to find out is to ask the staff who will be doing the job. Experienced technology support staff can often estimate the time needed to specify, select, and implement a new product based on their previous experience with similar implementations. You can also ask the technology vendor. The vendors should be able to give you a good estimate of the amount of time needed for each possible project, based on their previous experiences with other clients.

If you are considering sustaining or expanding an existing service, the needs assessment and selection stages may be quite short. But don't forget that even an expansion project will result in an increase in the workload at the maintenance stage. The library's experience with the product or service to date will be a reasonable indicator of the increased maintenance stage requirements you can expect from an expanded service.

If the product or service under consideration is unlike anything your staff has undertaken before, they may have difficulty estimating the time required. One possibility is to

FIGURE 22
Example of Workform 12, Project Time Estimates

Project Name: Replace Pentium 133s

STEPS	DAYS REQUIRED FOR EACH STEP	TOTAL DAYS FOR EACH PHASE
Needs Assessment		
Define minimum configuration and software required	½ day	
Total, Needs Assessment Phase		½ day
Selection		
Get quotes from 2–3 suppliers	1 day	
Prepare "justification for selection" paperwork	½ day	
Get final approvals and place order	1 day	
Total, Selection Phase		2 ½ days
Implementation		
Unbox and set up 5 PCs	½ day	
Install and configure software	1 day	
Deinstall P133s and install new machines at branch	¾ day	
Total, Implementation Phase		2 ¼ days
Retirement		
Complete deaccessioning paperwork on P133s and ship to resale center	½ day	
Total, Retirement Phase		½ day
Total for Project		5 ¾ days
Maintenance Phase: no increase in # of supported PCs		No change

ask the vendor for estimates. You might also call staff from other libraries that have already implemented the service or are currently offering the product. They will probably be able to give you reasonable estimates of the implementation time.

Another possibility is to do a pilot project in order to help the technology staff estimate the requirements of a full-scale implementation. A pilot project is a controlled mini-implementation of a larger-scale project. For example, you might install a publicly available wireless Internet connection at only one branch and test it before you commit to rolling out public wireless access at all your service points. A pilot project is one way to develop accurate estimates of the needs assessment, selection, implementation, and maintenance phase requirements. It can also help you determine the true costs of a new technology. A pilot project can help ensure that you have whatever security the technology might require in place before you make the technology available in multiple locations.

A pilot project also gives you a chance to test your public relations associated with the project and to identify what staff training will be needed in support of the new service.

Finally, a pilot project is a way to determine if you need to make adjustments to your assumptions about how well the product or service meets the service objectives it is intended to support. This can save you from spending a lot of time and money on a service or product the public really isn't interested in using. A pilot project will also provide a way to test your assumptions about the efficiency of certain products. It may be that the projected staff time savings never materialize. Again, it is better to discover this before you have made a significant investment in the product.

Summarize Your Findings

By now you have a lot of information about the technology-supported projects and services you are considering. You know which strategic plan service objective each project or service will address. You have projected costs and estimates of the time it will take to implement each possible project. You know whether or not your technology, support services staff, and public services staff currently have the skills needed to accomplish the project. It may be easier to make choices from among the available options if you summarize the key points of each technology-supported project or service on a single form. Workform 13, Summary of Projects, provides a format you can use to gather all the important data together in a single place. (See figure 23.)

FIGURE 23
Workform 13, Summary of Projects—Example 1

A. Project Name	B. Service Objective or Admin/Staff	C. Sustain, Expand, or New	D. Estimated Cost	E. Days to Complete	F. Skills Available
P133 replacements	Goal 3: Information Literacy Goal 4: General Reference	Sustain	$7,500	5½ days	Ruth
Digital projector for Ash branch computer lab	Goal 3: Information Literacy	New	$2,100	1 day	Tim

Rather than completing the written workform, you may find it more useful to use Workform 13 as a template for building an electronic spreadsheet or database that you can easily sort and resort as you evaluate the data you have gathered. For example, you can sort the projects by the estimated time needed to complete them, separating those that will be relatively easy to accomplish from those that will be quite challenging.

How do you identify an easy project? "Easy" means something different for each library. If your staff already have all the skills needed to implement and use the technology, you might consider that to be an easy project, especially if it won't take much time to complete. If your staff have the necessary skills to implement and use the project, but completing the project will take more than 50 percent of all the technical support staff's time that is available, you would probably judge it to be challenging. Of course, if you don't have the skills on staff to begin with, then even a short-duration project will be a challenge. Once you have decided which category each project falls into, record your decision on Workform 13. You will return to your decisions here later as you select projects for the final plan.

Does all this mean you shouldn't do the challenging projects? No, of course not. If a challenging project really meets your service objectives and you have judged that it will be highly appealing to your target audience, then implementing that project may be a good investment. In similar fashion, if the project will result in significant staff efficiencies, it may be a good investment. Don't shy away from the challenges: just recognize them, include the necessary training in your budget, and allow for the staff learning curve in your implementation timelines.

Another way to sort the options you are evaluating is by the cost of the projects. This will help you distinguish between costly and inexpensive or reasonably priced projects. Again, "costly" means something different in each library. A project that costs $40,000 won't seem as costly to a library with a $2 million budget as it will to a library with a $400,000 budget. Even if the costs seem reasonable compared to the library's overall budget, the library probably can't fund everything the technology committee is considering. You have to make judgments about project costs. If one project costs significantly more than another, do you expect that you would achieve greater results from the more costly project? Would the increased results warrant the extra expenditure?

If the costs seem insurmountable, you still don't have to give up. If the costly project targets multiple service objectives and would answer the needs of your users in a way no other option would, be creative about looking for money. This is particularly true if the maintenance stage costs are not high and you just find the implementation costs daunting. Maybe the library director and the board can use the data the technology planning committee has gathered in a fund-raising effort. Surely any grant application you fill out for funding will be made easier by the work you've done to this point.

Again, once you have decided whether each project is inexpensive or costly, record your decision on Workform 13. Your decisions on which projects make the final plan in Step 7.2, Choose from among Expansion and New Projects (see the next chapter), will depend in part on this information.

For those projects that you expect will increase the library's efficiency, compare the projected costs to the expected savings that you developed on Workform 6, Evaluating Efficiency Projects: Staff Savings. If the project will cost more than you expect to save, you will probably want to drop it from further consideration unless it dramatically improves customer service. Similarly, if the payback period is longer than the expected life of the technology itself, drop the project from further consideration. Improving the efficiency of the targeted activity may still be an important goal, but the projects you have identified aren't the right ones. Their costs are too high. You will need to rethink your approach to the problem or search for other, less costly technical solutions. If you adopt the recommendations of chapter 6 and make technology planning an ongoing process in your library, you soon will have the opportunity to reconsider these projects during your regular review of technology issues.

Part 3 of the Tree County Public Library case study illustrates that portion of the planning process discussed in this chapter.

What's Next?

When you have sorted the easy from challenging, the inexpensive from the costly, and dropped the efficiency projects that didn't pay out in a reasonable time, you are left with a group of great projects. Can you fund them all? Probably not, so it is time to move on to Task 7, Select and Present.

CASE STUDY

TREE COUNTY PUBLIC LIBRARY

PART 3

Assessing Where We Are

The members of the technology planning committee have been discussing the resource requirements for their recommended technology-supported public services and projects that would result in staff efficiencies. The list of "services to be sustained" developed by the planning committee and preliminarily approved by library administration gives the IT department a starting point for assessing the current infrastructure. Working with copies of Workform 7, Infrastructure Assessment, the IT staff develop an overview of existing and needed upgrades. Based on the planning committee's proposed recommendation, the IT staff agree that adding office automation software to some of the OPAC-only stations is a needed upgrade and will result in improved services. They summarize their findings on Workform 9, Costs to Sustain Services, for the planning committee to review.

For each new project, the IT staff contact potential suppliers of the technology, identifying the cost and skills needed. They also complete a copy of Workform 12, Project Time Estimates, based on their own experience and what they learn from the vendors for each project.

Finally, the IT manager summarizes the required technical skills and identifies which staff members have those skills on Workform 11, Technical Skills Needed. She also projects how many total hours of staff time are available to work on projects after the needs of ongoing maintenance are addressed. Copies of Workforms 8–12 are sent to each committee member before the next meeting.

NOTES

1. The checklists are available at http://www.rrlc.org/competencies/techcomp.html.
2. The survey is available at http://techsurveyor.npower.org/techsurveyor/staff_skills.asp.
3. Sandra Nelson, Ellen Altman, and Diane Mayo, *Managing for Results: Effective Resource Allocation for Public Libraries* (Chicago: American Library Association, 2000), 41.

Chapter 4

Choose and Inform

It is decision-making time. Time to choose from among all the options you have been working with and recommend certain projects for inclusion in the library's technology plan. The good news is that the process to this point has left you with nothing but good projects to choose from. You have already dropped the projects that didn't link to your service plan, cost more than you could expect to save by implementing them, or required more staff resources than you have to devote to your technology. The bad news is that everything left under consideration is a good project. How do you choose from among them? Even if your library can afford both the money and the staff time to do them all (lucky you!), how do you set priorities to make sure you get the most important projects done first?

TASK 7: SELECT AND PRESENT

The best way to choose from a number of projects is to apply a succession of criteria filters to them. Starting with the criterion that is most important, judge all of the projects against that criterion and add the projects that met that criterion to the plan. Apply the next level of filter to the remaining projects. Again, add the projects that meet the criterion to the plan. Then move on to the third filter and so on, until you have as many projects as you can reasonably do in the next year. When you run out of resources (staff time and money) to assign to the projects, you are done with the plan. If you are trying to develop a multiyear plan, once you have filled the first year with projects, continue through the process for the second year. Note that technologies change too fast to make planning more than two or three years in advance worthwhile.

Step 7.1
Begin with Needed Investments to Sustain
Current Levels of Service

The first filter you will apply is the "current services" filter. Sort the entries on Workform 13, Summary of Projects, to identify those marked as "sustain" projects. (See figure 24.) This is your first set of projects to consider. Add up the costs and the amount of time needed to accomplish these projects. Answer the following question:

> *Are the total costs less than your annual budget for technology investments?*

If the answer is yes, then move on to the next question.

If the answer is no, or you don't have a line item in the operational budget for technology expenditures, then you will need to decide which "sustain" projects have the highest priority and plan to do them first. Perhaps some of the listed projects are prerequisites for other projects on the expansion or new projects list. Maybe you will lose vendor support for mission-critical software or hardware if you don't get a particular project done within a specific time frame. Review the Issues and Dependencies section of Workform 7, Infrastructure Assessment, to see what you identified earlier.

If there is nothing that clearly gives one or more of these sustain projects priority over the others, then return to the library's strategic service plan for guidance in prioritizing projects. The library's service goals are ranked in order of importance, so you can sort the "sustain" projects by service goal to develop a prioritized list of the public services projects on your list. Break a tie between multiple projects that meet the same goal by giving a higher ranking to projects that will help you meet multiple service goals.

Your list probably also includes some administrative function projects needed to sustain the library's daily operations. You need some way to prioritize these projects, which aren't linked to service goals, in relation to the public service projects on your list. The question to ask yourself in ranking administrative function projects is, "If we don't do this, will it negatively affect our ability to deliver services to our customers?" If the answer is yes, then sustaining the technologies that support that administrative function should get a top priority ranking. The best public service technology doesn't outrank the basic tools needed to keep the library operating. You may decide to defer adding new administrative technologies or expanding current ones in favor of public service technologies, but once you have committed to a technology-based administrative function, you need to sustain it; only rarely can you go back to the old manual way of doing things.

Figure 24 is an example of ranking administrative and service "sustain" projects together. Upgrading the network to support the payroll system ranks higher than replacing the public PCs. If you can't pay the staff, they won't be around to serve the public. But the committee decided that the e-mail server could limp along longer than the public PCs and gave it the third priority.

FIGURE 24
Workform 13, Summary of Projects—Example 2

A. Project Name	B. Service Objective or Admin/Staff	C. Sustain, Expand, or New	D. Estimated Cost	E. Days to Complete	F. Skills Available
Establish VPN to payroll service	Admin	Sustain	$4,000	4 days	Vendor
P133 replacements	Goal 3: Information Literacy Goal 4: General Reference	Sustain	$7,500	5½ days	Ruth
Replace e-mail server	Admin	Sustain	$3,500	4 days	Tim

Using the list of "sustain" projects and the criteria described earlier, sort your projects in priority order. You will use that order when evaluating the answer to the next question:

Do you have enough staff time available to implement these projects?

Look at the total number of days or weeks these projects will take to complete. Think back to the number of hours the technology support staff estimated were available for project implementation during Step 6.2. If the days needed to complete the projects exceed the days available, you will have to make some adjustments or set some priorities. Perhaps there are stages of a project where staff other than the technical support staff can participate, reducing the actual time the technology staff need to expend on the projects. Even though your staff has the skills, you may want to hire the vendor to do the work so that your staff can concentrate on the things only they can do.

If you make adjustments in the estimated time to complete the projects, be sure to write down the logic behind those adjustments. Your adjustments are actually a set of conditions that need to be met before the projects can proceed as planned. Part of the final approval process will be gaining everyone's agreement that those conditions will be met.

If you can't find a way to make the days required be less than or equal to the days available, then you have to prioritize the projects. Prerequisites for other projects, a looming lack of vendor support or other external deadlines you can't control, a ranking of the service goals supported, and the mission-critical nature of the administrative functions to be sustained are all criteria you can apply to prioritize the projects. If you started this portion of the selection process with a prioritized list, the point at which the needed days exceed the available days is the cutoff for your first year's plan. Figure 25 shows an example of a prioritized list that exceeds the library staff's available time to implement it. The jagged horizontal line marks the point at which the planning committee had to stop adding projects to the first year of the plan due to lack of staff availability to manage projects.

FIGURE 25
Example of Prioritized List of Technology Projects

**Workform 13,
Summary of Projects**

A. Project Name		E. Days to Complete*
Upgrade Windows 2000 desktops to Windows XP		20 days
Upgrade ILS software, including configuring, testing, and loading new client software and training staff on changes		15 days
Replace circulation receipt printers		8 days
Replace self-check machines with newer generation of hardware		10 days
Replace children's CD network with website links to licensed resources		4 days
Upgrade MS Office applications to Office 2005, including training staff on changes		25 days
Total Time Needed		**82 days**

Time available: 60 days

* Remember that the Days to Complete column represents the IT staff hours needed to accomplish each project, not the elapsed time from start to finish of the entire project.

If you've got the money and the time to sustain your current infrastructure and still have dollars and hours left over, then you can move on to considering expansion or new projects. If you've already "spent" the available time and money, you are done and can move on to Step 7.3.

Step 7.2
Choose from among Expansion and New Projects

Return to the Workform 13, Summary of Projects list, this time searching for the expanded or new services projects. There are several criteria filters you can apply to the projects in this group. The first two criteria you might want to apply are whether the projects are *required by law* and whether they are *politically advantageous.*

Projects that are required by law include things you need to do to be in compliance with laws such as the Americans with Disabilities Act or CIPA. Politically advantageous projects are those that make integration with other city or county departments easier, e.g., adopting new group calendaring, accounting, or human resources systems. While it might not be your first choice to spend your limited money and technology staff time on the politically advantageous ones, if you ignore or short-staff these types of projects, you risk the ire of senior managers and politicians in your community. It is better to just schedule them, do them, and move on.

The filters you have applied thus far are inclusive criteria—if the project meets the criterion and you have the resources to do it, it is in the plan. Now you are going to categorize and prioritize the remaining projects to select from among them.

Sort the remaining projects into three categories: support for service objectives, administrative function projects, and other. You will apply filters to each group to rank the projects in order of the benefits received by doing them.

SUPPORT FOR SERVICE OBJECTIVES

The filter most commonly applied to projects that will help you meet your service objectives is *progress toward achieving the highest-priority service objectives.* Again, turn to the library's service objectives. Rank the expanded and new projects in service goal priority order.

ADMINISTRATIVE FUNCTION PROJECTS

The filter most commonly applied to administrative function or efficiency projects is *return on investment.* Return on investment (ROI) is a calculation of the dollars saved by the project divided by the dollars expended on it. A result of greater than 1 means you will save more than you spend. A result of less than 1 means you'll spend more than you save. The higher the result, the more the return you'll get from your investment.

For example, a project that will save the library $6,000 in staff time and third-party costs will cost $3,000 to implement. The formula is:

$$\frac{\$ \text{ saved}}{\$ \text{ spent}} = \text{ROI} \qquad \text{or} \qquad \frac{\$6,000}{\$3,000} = 2.0$$

There may be administrative projects on your list with a very low ROI that you have decided to consider because a consequence of implementing them is the potential for improving customer service. There may even be projects with an ROI of zero (no measurable cost savings at all). If you retain such projects in your plan, be sure you have a good explanation of the expected customer benefits to outweigh the lack of return on investment.

OTHER

This last category generally covers best IT practices. These projects usually fall in the administration function group of projects and may include such things as organizing wiring closets, documenting installed systems, or developing disaster plans. They don't often involve great outlays of money and have little quantifiable cost savings benefits, but they require technology support staff time to execute. These are the types of projects, like cleaning your desk or your junk room at home, that always get put off because there is something more pressing that needs to be done. Just as you occasionally do need to break down and clean the desk because you can't find anything on it, sometimes these "right thing to do" projects have to rise to the top so the technology support staff can continue to function.

Let the technology support staff filter this group and set the order of priority. They know which of these issues is causing them the biggest headaches.

CHOOSING

Once you are done ranking each of these three types of projects, you need to decide how many of each type you will put in the plan. Again, the first question is how much time and money do you have left to spend? If you have eighteen days of technology staff project management time left, you shouldn't choose projects that represent more than eighteen days' worth of work in the next year. If you only have $25,000 left in the budget, you shouldn't plan to spend more than that.

Once you acknowledge the limitations of available budget and staff, then picking the group you choose from first is a function of your own internal operating environment and objectives. In difficult budget times, administrative efficiency projects often take priority over expanded or new services. In stable budget periods, many libraries will try to balance their expenditures for operating efficiencies and their investments for their service objectives. When additional revenues become available, most libraries will try to spend at least a portion of those funds investing in new service priorities.

Another set of factors you will want to include is the easy or challenging and inexpensive or costly determinations the committee made at the end of Task 6, Determine the Requirements of New or Expanded Services. Everyone in the library, from the board to the members of the planning committee to the IT staff who must implement the plan, will need to be able to celebrate some successes as the result of the plan. Choosing only one or two costly projects will limit the opportunities to do so. Choosing a larger number of inexpensive projects that also meet your service objectives probably will give more people a chance to benefit from the plan.

If you choose only hard projects, you run the risk that the IT staff will burn out in the course of the implementation period. Everyone needs to balance really hard work with easier tasks that offer the opportunity to feel successful. A combination of hard and easy projects will give the IT staff some needed variety in their work tasks.

Step 7.3
Write up Decisions with Rationale and Anticipated Outcomes;
Provide Estimated Budgets and Timelines

The planning committee's work is almost done. All your hard work has brought you to the point where you have a set of recommended technology investments that will support the library's service plan. You may also be recommending projects that control or reduce operating costs or that introduce new administrative functions. It is possible that you have identified currently installed technologies that are no longer appropriate for the library's service objectives and that can be phased out or redirected to a more important use.

The committee chair or one or two designated committee members should be charged with writing up the committee's results. This summary of your efforts and decisions will be the basis of your presentation to whoever will approve and adopt your plan. It will also provide the information needed to present the plan to the audiences that were identified way back in Step 1.1.

Format the report in whatever narrative style is standard for your organization. Some libraries use a "just the facts, ma'am" bullet-item report format. Others prefer a fuller, more descriptive narrative that captures the process as well as the results. Whichever format works in your library, the data elements you need to include are

> *A list of the recommended projects in priority order, and by year if you are developing a multiyear plan.* In the list, separate the projects needed to sustain existing services from the expanded or new projects in order to make this distinction clear for all readers.

> *The estimated cost of implementation and the estimated amount of staff time required for each project.* If the committee made any adjustments to the staffing requirements of a project during its deliberations in Step 7.1 (e.g., including non-IT staff in the project, or expecting that a portion of the needed time will be purchased from a vendor), be sure to include these conditions in the write-up of the project. If the project will require significant training of other staff, include an estimate of the training time that may be involved in the implementation, along with the IT staff time estimates.

> *Information about the specific service objectives each project supports for both sustaining and new or expanded service objective projects.*

> *Expected return on investment and the payback period for efficiency projects, or expected customer service consequences for those projects with a low or nonexistent ROI.*

> *A summary of the budget required, by year, to support the committee's complete set of recommendations.*

> *A section on those technologies the committee is recommending phasing out, with a brief explanation of why you believe they are no longer needed.*

Figure 26 is a sample table of contents for a technology plan. Elements I through V should be included in any plan. Optional additions VI and VII just present the data in another format, making it easier for the reader to see the year-by-year project lists and the complete set of recommendations by service goal. Use these additions if you believe they will be of interest to your audiences.

If you have completed the plan within the constraints of available staff time or budget dollars and there are still great projects that didn't make it to the plan, consider optional addition VIII, a section that includes information about these projects. If you bring these projects to the attention of others, perhaps a grant opportunity will be discovered, or maybe additional funds will become available during the budget year.

FIGURE 26
Example of Technology Plan Table of Contents

Basic Plan

I. Introduction

> Includes brief background on the planning process and current state of technology-based services
>
> Describes the differences between sustain, expand, and new projects
>
> Defines "public service" and "administrative function"

II. List of Recommended "Sustain" Projects in Priority Order

> One entry for each project, including:
>
> - Benefits to the organization, e.g., service goals or administrative functions supported
> - Anticipated costs and return on investment, if any
> - Staff time required to implement, including any adjustments made during deliberations
> - Year of the plan in which the project will be implemented (1st or 2nd)

III. List of Recommended Expanded and New Projects in Priority Order

> One entry for each project, including:
>
> - Benefits to the organization, e.g., service goals supported, administrative functions supported
> - Anticipated costs and return on investment, if any
> - Staff time requirements to implement, including any adjustments made during deliberations
> - Year of the plan in which the project will be implemented (1st or 2nd)

IV. Cost Summary of All Recommendations

> By year for a multiyear plan

V. List of Recommended Phaseout Projects

> One entry for each project, including an explanation of why the recommendation is made

Optional Additions

VI. Year-by-Year Timeline of Recommended Projects

> Includes any projects currently under way

VII. Summary of Recommended Projects Listed by Service Goal

VIII. List of Good Projects Not Included in the Plan

> Include benefits to the organization, estimated costs, and staff time needed

---

Once the summary report is written, all the members of the committee should review it before it is sent on to the organization.

Step 7.4
Present as Needed to Decision Makers for Approval and Commitment to Funding

Unless your staff is small enough that everyone participated in the planning process, there will be several people anxiously awaiting the recommendations of the committee. Library administrators, the people who need to find the funds to make the plan happen, will need to see the plan.

Funding the Plan

As you finished the planning process and realized just how much money would be required to fully implement the recommended projects, you were probably somewhat startled by the total. If the committee was working with a budgeted amount available, then there are probably a number of good projects in the "projects we didn't select" section of the committee's report. If you didn't have a target budget amount, you understand that the plan may get trimmed to match the available funding at some point. There is no question that the costs to implement a plan like this can add up quickly. However, it is important not to get discouraged by the total resources required. The library can obtain the needed resources from a variety of sources.

Reallocating Existing Resources

Libraries tend to assume that all new programs and services must be funded with new resources. However, in today's funding environment, many libraries are realizing that to obtain the resources they need for new programs, they are going to have to reallocate funds from existing programs and services. All government funding is being scrutinized more carefully than ever before by taxpayers convinced that public services should be "leaner and meaner." Libraries are not exempt from this scrutiny, and, as librarians and board members know all too well, many public libraries are already operating with fewer resources than they need to accomplish everything they are being asked to do. This creates a very difficult situation for those responsible for obtaining and allocating the resources required to operate the library. There is no question that it is more pleasant to create new programs and services than it is to modify or discontinue programs that are no longer as effective as they once were.

Everyone needs to be very aware of the impact of the technology plan you have just completed on the library's current services and programs. For example, if the plan focuses on adding customer self-service functions such as self-service renewals, self-checkout stations, and a self-service PC reservation system, how will that impact the staff you need at the public desks? If you are adding an acquisitions module to your integrated library system, what paper files can you get rid of? How will the flow of information between selectors and acquisitions staff change? We all know of libraries that maintain paper files even after automation has made them redundant. Think of libraries that still have vertical files when the world's biggest vertical file, the Internet, is just a keystroke away! When asked why, these libraries provide a variety of answers (most are versions of the old belt-and-suspenders story), but the real answer is that they find it impossible to let go of the old when they implement the new. This is a luxury that libraries cannot afford as the pace of change accelerates and the cost of adapting to those changes increases. The libraries that succeed in this new environment will be those that replace and adapt their services, not the libraries that simply try to add endless new programs and services with no modification of their existing environment.

Requesting New Funds from Your Funding Body

It is unlikely that you will be able to fully implement your technology plan by reallocating your current resources, nor should you expect to. As you implement your technology plan, you will probably be making significant investments in equipment and software. You may also need to upgrade your facility to accommodate your selected technology infrastructure. Your first source of funding for many of these items will be your local funding body. Requests for funding for technology enhancements may be received more positively by your funding body than other kinds of library requests. Sometimes it is difficult to convince people that additional funds are needed for materials or that you need new staff for a special program. However, the library is not the only local governmental agency that is being affected by technology. Many, if not most, of the other city or county departments have automated their services. This is an area of expenditure that the members of your funding body are likely to understand and recognize as inevitable.

Most governmental funding bodies provide two kinds of appropriations: onetime or nonrecurring appropriations and ongoing or recurring appropriations. When you prepare your budget request, you will want to think carefully about whether to request nonrecurring or recurring funds.

Nonrecurring funds. In the past, many libraries funded their automation purchases, both large and small, from onetime appropriations. However, as technology becomes integrated into every aspect of library service, this is no longer an appropriate funding strategy, any more than it would be to fund your materials budget with onetime monies. What kind of expenditures should you make from onetime appropriations? It is certainly appropriate to fund building renovations, additional electrical service, upgraded data cabling, etc., from onetime monies. It is also possible to purchase the computer furniture you need from nonrecurring funds. After all, the probable life span of the furniture is a lot longer than the probable life span of the equipment it will hold or the software that will run on the equipment. Finally, if one or more of your selected technology projects requires a significant initial investment but can be maintained from a much smaller ongoing investment, it may be possible to make the initial investment from onetime funds, with the clear understanding that there will be ongoing costs associated with the project and that those will be budgeted from recurring funds.

Recurring funds. Many of the costs associated with your technology plan are best funded with recurring funds. As the sustaining projects in your plan demonstrate, libraries need to replace or upgrade their hardware and software regularly. Clearly, technology is an ongoing expense, just as your materials budget and staff costs are. You want to work with representatives from your funding body to establish a new or expanded technology category in your operating budget if you don't have such a category now.

Using Funds Provided by Friends of the Library or Library Foundation

Many public libraries have library Friends groups that hold fund-raising activities and provide resources for special projects. More and more libraries are also establishing library foundations to manage fund-raising activities. Either of these groups could be a source of some of the funds you will need to implement your technology plan. However, if you intend to ask the Friends or foundation to support your plan, you will probably want to involve them in the planning process early on. You may not want to have a member of the Friends or the foundation board to serve on the planning committee, and they probably won't want to spend that much time or be involved in that level of detail. However, you will want to keep them informed about the planning process and the decisions being made at each step of that process. By doing that, you will ensure that there are no surprises on either side. The Friends or foundation will have a clear understanding of what they are being asked to support because they will have followed the process. This in turn should mean that the library will be able to rely on the funding being available when it is needed.

One new trend in foundation funding is establishing endowments to fund future purchases. Many library foundations have established endowments for books; some are also beginning to establish endowments for technology. Endowments invest onetime monies in order to provide recurring funds from the proceeds of the investment.

The issues surrounding recurring and nonrecurring funds that were discussed previously also apply here. Some Friends groups and library foundations are quite well endowed and can commit to ongoing support for a project. Others rely on annual fund-raising activities such as book sales or author dinners and are more comfortable making onetime commitments. The kinds of things that you might fund with monies provided by Friends or a library foundation will depend on the type of funding available.

Obtaining Outside Grant Funds

There is a wide variety of grant opportunities available to help libraries implement technology plans. The federal Library Services and Technology Act (LSTA), which was passed by Congress in 1996 and renewed as a section of the Museum and Library Services Act of 2003, focuses on helping libraries use technology to improve library services. The renewed act has six priorities:

1. Expand services for learning and access to information and educational resources in a variety of formats, in all types of libraries, for individuals of all ages.
2. Develop library services that provide all users access to information through local, state, regional, national, and international electronic networks.
3. Provide electronic and other linkages between and among all types of libraries.
4. Develop public and private partnerships with other agencies and community-based organizations.
5. Target library services to individuals of diverse geographic, cultural, and socioeconomic backgrounds, to individuals with disabilities, and to individuals with limited functional literacy or information skills.

6. Target library and information services to persons having difficulty using a library and to underserved urban and rural communities, including children from families with incomes below the poverty line (as defined by the Office of Management and Budget).[1]

The Library Services and Technology Act provides funding to state library agencies in all fifty states, most of which in turn provide grants to libraries within their states. Every public library should be familiar with the grant opportunities available from its state library agency. If you need further information, you can call your state library agency or check its website. The Wisconsin State Library Division of the Wisconsin Department of Public Instruction maintains a web listing of all fifty state library agencies at http://www .dpi.state.wi.us/dpi/dlcl/pld/statelib.html. For more information on the Library Services and Technology Act, check out the website maintained by the Institute of Museum and Library Services at http://www.imls.fed.us.

There are many other grant opportunities to help you implement your technology plan. When considering possible funding, it often pays to start at the local level. Are there local organizations or corporations that might be interested in providing some of the resources you need? You might want to ask the Lions Club for the funding you need to purchase special software for the visually impaired. A local corporation might be interested in supporting a literacy center or a job skills program. You may find that the local chamber of commerce can help you find funding for providing technology-based services to your small business community.

There are many sources of grant funds available to public libraries, but every potential funder will have different priorities and a different application process. The good news is that the technology plan you have developed using *Technology for Results* should provide all the information you need to complete any grant application you decide to submit. Just remember that the issues surrounding recurring and nonrecurring funds continue to apply here. Grant funders are very aware of the ongoing costs of projects, and one of the things they will be looking for in your application is a clear understanding of the appropriate uses of onetime funding and the ways that you intend to provide the necessary continuing support for the purchases made with grant funding.

Taking Advantage of Discounts and Special Rates

Another source of support for portions of your technology plan may be found in special or reduced rates on equipment, software, or telecommunications charges that are made available to public libraries. One of the best-known examples of these kinds of special rates is the Universal Service portion of the Telecommunications Act of 1996. This provides discounts for eligible schools and libraries on all commercially available telecommunication services, Internet access, and internal connections, including local area networks. Discounts can range from 20 to 90 percent depending on economic need. For current information on the application process for Universal Service funds, check with the Federal Communications Commission at http://www.fcc.gov/learnnet. In addition to the Universal Service discounts, many state public utility or public service commissions have passed special statewide telecommunication discounts for libraries and educational institutions. Many of these have been modified based on the Universal Service legislation, but it would probably be worth checking with your state library agency to see if any special state telecommunications discounts are available.

CompuMentor, a nonprofit technology assistance organization, operates TechSoup.org, a technology website for nonprofits that features content and dialogue from the nonprofit and technology communities. Their TechSoup Stock service is a discount technology store for the nonprofit community that distributes contributions from leading technology providers like Microsoft and Symantec.

Finally, remember that some equipment and software vendors provide discounts for library and educational institutions. It never hurts to ask.

Are There Resources Other Than Money That Would Be Useful?

Libraries often think of resources solely in terms of financial aid. However, there may be other kinds of resources that could be very valuable to you as you implement your technology plan. For example, local computer stores may be willing to donate some hardware or software in return for public acknowledgment of their contribution. If you are operating with very limited funds, you may want to talk to the advanced woodworking class at your local high school about making computer tables.

Finally, consider asking for volunteers to help you introduce the public to any new technologies you install. For instance, if you make web page development software available to the public, you might recruit a group of web writers (try high school students) to help the staff during the critical first month or two.

The most important things to remember when trying to obtain the resources you need to implement your technology plan are to be flexible and to be creative. It is also critical that you approach this task with a positive attitude. If you believe that there is no way you can fund the technology-based services and programs your library needs, you will be right—that kind of negative attitude is almost always a self-fulfilling prophecy. Focus instead on the positive. You have just completed a process that has resulted in a well-documented and fully justified plan for using technology to provide quality information services to the people of your community. This plan includes everything you need to make a compelling argument for support from your funding body and from outside grant providers, but you won't get what you need if you don't ask.

TASK 8: INFORM

The people on the committee who have been immersed in the planning process are often so close to the process that they forget that others don't know as much about it as they do. After the plan has been reviewed and endorsed by the library's executive team, it is time to let the rest of the organization know what your recommendations are.

Step 8.1
Present the Adopted Plan to Target Audiences

There will be a variety of audiences for information on the plan. These might include your library board, governing officials, the city or county manager, and the city or county IT department. Most of these audiences were identified at the very beginning of the planning process in Workform 1, but you may have discovered others during the process that expressed an interest in the results.

Identify the different audiences you need to reach. Consider what it is you want the members of each specific audience to do. Are you just providing information or do you need their approval to proceed with the plan? If you need approvals, think about what possible questions or concerns they might have and include the answers to those questions in your initial presentation.

Begin your communication activities by making the presentations you need to make to audiences that have to approve the plan. There is no point in making a general announcement to all staff until you know the plan has been approved. The library director and the committee chair should work together to plan and deliver the needed presentations. After the final approvals are received, let the staff know what is happening.

Even if you originally informed the staff about the technology planning project, you'll need to remind them of it and let them know that it's been completed. Make sure everyone knows what you recommended and what the next steps will be in terms of implementation.

Staff will want a fairly detailed explanation of the process and your conclusions, especially if you weren't able to include all of the projects they suggested in the plan. Be prepared to describe the process, the criteria you applied to select the projects you did, and what may happen to the projects that weren't selected or have not yet been funded (e.g., further consideration if funding becomes available, seeking grant funds, or the next round of planning). Staff will also be very interested in the timelines for when all this is going to happen. All you will know at this point is which year of the plan each project will be scheduled, but this is a great time for the IT staff to discuss their project management processes and to let the staff know how the project implementations will be scheduled.

The board will want to know about the services your plan will support, the time or money the efficiency projects will save, and what it is all going to cost. The city or county IT department will be interested in the technologies you are looking at and will be particularly interested in any "politically advantageous" projects you included. The city manager will want at most a very distilled communication. A basic rule of thumb is that the higher in level or status the person you want to communicate with is, the less time and patience they have to focus on your communication. They want to cut to the chase: what you are doing, the reasons why (briefly!), and how much (usually money, but also possibly people, time, or other resources). The politicians will also want a distilled communication, but they are usually looking for anecdotes about how your plan will affect real people. For them the message might be "100 more children each month will be able to work on their information retrieval skills" rather than "we'll be adding ten PCs in the Children's Room."

Everyone is busy and overloaded with information today. Learning how to convey the information that the receiver needs with sufficient but not extraneous explanation is a skill worth developing. Too often staff members and managers react to this feeling of being overloaded by saying that they don't want more communication. That really isn't what they mean, which you find out the minute you don't communicate about something that affects them. Defining your audiences and identifying what you want them to do are techniques that will help you in crafting communications that will work both for you and for those you're trying to communicate with.

Step 8.2
Inform the Public

The public will also be interested in the outcome of your planning process, especially as it affects their services. In general the public will be less interested in the technical details and more interested in the expected results.

Many libraries produce a simple tri-fold flyer with the highlights of the plan as it affects their service objectives. The staff and administrative projects are usually of less interest to the public, but if your community is experiencing fiscally tough times, the public may appreciate knowing about steps you have taken to control costs.

You are communicating about a technology plan, so be sure to take advantage of the technology-based forms of communication you have at your disposal, such as your website, a library blog, or an electronic newsletter if you produce one.

Part 4 of the Tree County Public Library case study illustrates that part of the planning process discussed in this chapter.

CASE STUDY

TREE
COUNTY
PUBLIC
LIBRARY

PART 4

Making Decisions

Prior to the meeting to decide which projects will be prioritized and recommended for funding, the committee chair creates a spreadsheet modeled on Workform 13, Summary of Projects. The spreadsheet summarizes all the data developed to date. She brings her laptop, a digital projector, and a printer to the meeting.

The planning committee begins by asking the chair to sort the spreadsheet by "sustain" projects, expand projects, and new projects. The estimated costs of all the sustain projects are totaled together. Fortunately, these projects cost considerably less than the $75,000 annual target the director gave them, and the estimated number of days to complete these projects is also less than the total number of days available.

The expand projects are totaled next. Added to the "sustain" projects, there is still money available for new projects, but the time available is becoming quite small.

The committee then focuses on the new projects. They determine that none of the possible projects falls into the "required by law" or "politically advantageous" categories. There are a few "right thing to do" projects that have the potential to free up some IT time. Even without freeing up staff time, there is enough time left to do three or four of the new projects. The remaining new public service projects are ranked by service goal. The administrative function projects are ranked by return on investment: projects with an ROI of greater than 1 are ranked first in order of their ROI, with the highest ranked first. These are followed by projects with an ROI of less than 1 but expected good customer service consequences. Finally, projects with ROIs of less than 1 and no customer service consequences are listed.

The top-ranked new public service project and the top-ranked new efficiency project are chosen, along with two of the right things to do. These last two are chosen because doing them will free nearly a complete full-time equivalent of IT staff in coming years. This will increase the number of projects that can be proposed for the following year.

The remaining new projects are ranked in the committee's recommended order of implementation and identified as possible second-year projects.

The committee chair thanks the group for a hard task well done and promises to send them the committee report with recommendations for review before the report is submitted to the library director.

NOTE

1. Library Services and Technology Act, http://www.imls.gov/grants/library/lib_gsla.asp.

Chapter 5

Implement

MILESTONES

By the time you finish this chapter you will know how to

- create a schedule for a technology implementation project
- phase in multiyear projectss
- monitor the progress of projects
- validate assumptions before proceeding with implementations

Having just a vision's no solution, everything depends on execution.
—Barbra Streisand, "Putting It Together"

The quote above captures an important thing you need to keep in mind about your new technology plan: the plan itself is not the objective. Implementing the plan is what it is all about.

TASK 9: IMPLEMENT THE PROJECTS IN THE PLAN

Planning and executing a technology implementation is generally the responsibility of the technology support staff. But it can, and usually does, involve staff from a wide range of functions throughout the library. Administrative staff participate in the procurement of the hardware and software; facilities people may need to prepare sites for new equipment; line staff are trained in using the new technologies and can then suggest the most effective ways to introduce the public to the service; and marketing staff develop press releases, customer handouts, and other supporting documentation for the project. With very few exceptions, a technology implementation is a multidimensional project that requires a structured approach and attentive oversight to stay on time and on budget. This means you need to take a project management approach to implementing the plan.

Step 9.1
Identify a Project Sponsor for Each Implementation

Someone in the organization needs to be assigned as the primary "customer" or "client" of the project. This person is called the "sponsor" and is usually not a member of the technology support staff. The logical choice is someone from the functional area that will be most affected by the project. Ideally, the sponsor will have been a member of the technology planning committee or will be the person who suggested the project for the planning committee's consideration. If neither of these is possible, then the sponsor needs to be someone who understands the objective of the project and agrees with that objective.

The project sponsor is the "go to" person when there are choices to be made during the implementation. The project sponsor is the contact point between the staff who are doing the technical implementation and the staff who will use the technology when it is installed. When parameters need to be established or indexing decisions are required, the technology support staff will turn to the project sponsor for decisions. In most cases, the project sponsor will solicit and coordinate the input of other staff who will use the technology to answer the necessary questions.

Step 9.2
Identify a Project Manager and Develop a Projected
Timeline with Needed Resources

The technology support staff assigns a project manager and develops a timeline for the project. Timeline development is not something that is dictated by technology support management, but is an interactive and iterative process with each project manager. The steps, in general, are as follows.

1. A technology support staffer is assigned to be the project manager.
2. The project manager prepares a narrative description and scope of his or her understanding of what the project does and does not include.
3. This narrative and scope is reviewed with his or her manager, the project sponsor, and maybe with the library's management. This step repeats until everyone agrees with the project scope.
4. The project manager prepares a list of steps that he or she thinks need to be done to accomplish the project. This list contains an estimate of how long each step will take and whether outside resources will be needed to accomplish each step (e.g., a server needs to be ordered or the telephone company needs to install some service). This step also repeats until everyone agrees with the timeline. The project sponsor will be involved at this stage as well, particularly as some of the steps in the process may be dependent on the sponsor's ability to provide needed information in a timely manner.
5. The project manager is now ready to start on the project.

The project manager and the project sponsor will work closely together throughout the implementation. Each person represents the other's point of contact in his or her department.

CREATING THE LIST OF STEPS

Experienced technology support staff develop timelines based on their experience with similar projects earlier in their careers. What do you do if your technology support staff doesn't have project experience, or if you don't have technology support staff? How do you manage the implementation of your plan?

The easiest way to approach a project is to divide the implementation process into subsets or stages. Each of these stages will be further divided into the steps required to accomplish the stage and the time each step will take to complete. Figure 27 is an example of a set of project stages.

FIGURE 27
Project Stages

	Implementation Stages	Duration	Responsible Party
1.	Needs Analysis	8 weeks	Project Mgr
2.	Procurement	12 weeks	Project Mgr
3.	Installation and Testing	8 weeks	Project Mgr

To determine the time needed to implement your overall plan, you will need to determine the duration of the steps in the needs analysis, procurement, and installation and testing stages of your plan.[1] If one step is site preparation, who will do the work, the city/county or an independent contractor? If it is an independent contractor, do you need to go to bid for those services, or do you simply have to schedule a time with your usual company? How long is it likely to take to complete the site preparation in each location? (Ask potential suppliers to estimate this for you.) Allow time in your planning for staff to review and test the work. For site preparation this testing could mean counting data outlets, plugging equipment into electrical outlets, or reviewing test data the installer has produced. For phone lines, it may mean passing data over the line. It is also wise to allow a little time for fixing problems. It is a rare project that doesn't require a little cleanup at the end.

Figure 28 is a set of stages with some steps added to each stage to identify needed actions. Note that this is just a sample of a project plan, not a list of durations that necessarily will apply to your own project planning.

FIGURE 28
Project Stages and Steps

	Implementation Stages	Duration	Responsible Party
1.	**Needs Analysis**	**8 weeks**	Project Mgr
	1.1 Meet with end users to discuss requirements	2 weeks	Project Mgr Sponsor
	1.2 Draft RFP	4 weeks	Project Mgr Sponsor
	1.3 Review and approve RFP	2 weeks	Project Mgr Sponsor Library Dir
2.	**Procurement**	**12 weeks**	Project Mgr Purchasing
	2.1 Issue RFP	4 weeks	Purchasing
	2.2 Evaluate responses	4 weeks	Project Mgr Sponsor
	2.3 Negotiate contract	4 weeks	Purchasing Project Mgr Sponsor
3.	**Installation and Testing**	**8 weeks**	Project Mgr
	3.1 Site preparation	4 weeks	Project Mgr Facilities
	3.2 Hardware installation and testing	1 week	Project Mgr
	3.3 Software installation and testing	3 weeks	Project Mgr Sponsor

In addition to determining the duration of each stage of the implementation, you need to decide which stages or steps are dependent on the completion of other stages or steps. For example, you can't install WAN equipment until you have telephone lines or cable TV connections to attach it to. Therefore, phone line or cable TV installation is a prerequisite for WAN equipment installation. You can't connect client PCs to a new system until the software is installed, and the software can't be installed and configured until the server is in place. So the server installation is a prerequisite to the software installation, and the hardware and software installations are both prerequisites for using the client PCs. If you determine that a step has a prerequisite, add the duration of the prerequisite step to the subsequent step to determine the overall duration for that stage. Another way to view a project schedule is to design a chart like the one shown in figure 29.

FIGURE 29
Project Schedule

	Wk. 1	Wk. 2	Wk. 3	Wk. 4	Wk. 5	Wk. 6	Wk. 7	Wk. 8
Order server	→———————————————————→							
Install and test server				→————→				
Load and test software					→————→			
Test client PC connectivity						→—————————————→		

Charting the stages of your implementation on a project schedule using either model shown above will help you determine how long it will take to fully implement each project in your plan. Your general objective should be to schedule the installation of equipment, phone lines, etc., as close as possible to the time when you will begin productive use of them. This is particularly true of elements with ongoing costs such as telecommunications services, software licenses, and hardware with monthly maintenance fees that begin upon installation. Paying for communication services, software licenses, or maintenance on equipment before you are able to make productive use of them wastes money. Buying a number of PCs before you have the site preparation completed to use them means you will have to find a place to store them and may mean that by the time you start to use them they have been superseded by a later model.

Sometimes you don't have control over the timing of your stages. Grant funds may have to be spent by a certain date even though unexpected delays in site preparation have delayed your project. But the general question to ask yourself as you are planning each step is, "When this step is completed, will we be ready to use the product or service we have installed and if not, why not?" Is it because you missed a prerequisite? Or is there another step that must be completed at the same time for you to begin to use the product? You will want to take these interdependencies into account as you plan the implementation.

PHASING THE IMPLEMENTATION OF YOUR PLAN

There are a number of reasons why you may want to implement the projects in your technology plan in phases. Your planning process may have identified the need to do a pilot project as a means of developing accurate estimates for the costs and support requirements of a larger project. You may need to fund a project with money that will become available in multiple budget years. Perhaps your plan includes a significant amount of staff training, both for the public services staff and for staff members who will manage your technology, and you want to complete at least the first round of training before you begin to install new products. You may have a small staff that only has time to master one new product at a time, or a technology support staff that must learn to manage and support a technology in a controlled environment before they can begin to manage it librarywide.

Whatever the reason, there are several ways you can phase in your technology plan. You can implement one product at a time, you can implement one facility at a time, or you can implement your plan at a minimal level of service and expand as funds become available or demand rises.

Phasing Implementation by Working in One Facility or Department at a Time

Sometimes the budget simply will not support the full implementation of infrastructure elements in every location at onetime. If you have a multibranch library, you might choose to phase a technology project by facility. If your library is in a single building and you need to phase in a project, you can phase it in by department. The only real exception to phasing within a building is in facilities upgrades: the installation of electricity and data cabling and increases in air conditioning. When you hire electricians or building contractors to rewire your building, the incremental costs of adding circuits or additional data cables is a fraction of the overall cost of the project. You should do all the site preparation for the ultimate environment you intend to support, even if it may take you several years to implement all of your activities.

Phasing Implementation by Installing the Minimum Required and Expanding Based on Demand

You can also phase your projects based on growth as demand rises or money for additional hardware or software becomes available. If you are introducing a new technology-based service for the first time, it may take a while for your public to develop an interest in it. In some projects, you can install the server, the network, and the software you have chosen; train the staff; and then phase in the number of user workstations you offer as public usage grows. If you have done complete site preparation in each facility, adding workstations is a relatively simple process involving purchasing, configuring, and installing the new equipment.

Step 9.3
Plan a Data-Capture Strategy to Measure Success

Every project you undertake needs to be evaluated for its success. Despite the care and attention you paid to selecting projects for the technology plan, 100 percent success with every project is rare. Rapidly changing technology and rapidly changing customer interests sometimes catch up with and surpass the implementation of your plans. Occasionally, you get too far in front of the public interest and a great idea just isn't ready for full-scale implementation yet. The early implementations of e-books are a great example. It took several different technological approaches before the publishing and library industries found a set of technologies that matched the public's interests. Now you can download electronic versions of print books to read on a variety of portable readers, log in to intensely indexed reference e-books that actually function more as databases, and access interactive and animated versions of classic children's titles online.

At the start of every project, the project manager and project sponsor need to discuss and agree on how the success of the project will be measured. The work done in the planning process will help. Each project was selected because it related to one of the library's service responses or because the planning committee believed that it would improve the efficiency or cost-effectiveness of library operations. Look to the committee's work for suggestions on what can be measured. Remember that your success measures should measure the results you achieve, not the inputs of your effort. The number of workstations installed is not a result; the number of hours of public service provided by them is.

The Results Series suggests three types of measures that can be collected to assess results. The first is a measure of the number of people served by a service or program. You can count people in one of two ways: you can count a person every time he or she uses a service (total number of users) or you can count a person once no matter how often he or she uses a service (total number of individuals served). For most technology implementations, the total number of users is easier to capture. Often the relative mix of on-site and off-site users is important as well.

The second type of measure determines how well a given service meets the needs of the people being served. This is done by asking the people receiving the service what they think in a survey, a focus group, or an interview. Online surveys are one way to query people's satisfaction with technology-based services.

The third category of measures concentrates on the number of service units or service transactions that are provided by the library. These include number of hours of service provided, number of downloads, number of customers authenticated, etc.

The measures you select need to be quantifiable, related to the objectives you are trying to achieve, and capable of being captured in a cost-effective way. These are the reasons why you need to have the discussion about what you want to measure early in the implementation process. Your measurement objectives could affect the products you choose or the approach you take in implementing the project.

Step 9.4
Report Regularly on Progress to All

Complex projects can easily get off schedule. Regular reporting on the status of each project ensures that slippage is noted early and opportunities to get the project back on track are identified.

Each week the project manager should prepare a status report for his or her projects. If a project is on schedule, this report can be as brief as "Project X is on schedule," since all the readers of the status report will have a copy of the expected timeline. If the project is ahead of schedule, the details need to be noted so that those affected will be prepared for the project sooner than they thought.

The project manager should also meet or communicate weekly with the project sponsor to discuss the status report. The weekly status reports should be distributed to the library's senior management and to the library's project prioritization committee, if one exists, in order to keep the entire organization aware of the implementation status of various projects.[2]

Of course, the reality is that projects tend to fall behind schedule. Why? People tend to be too optimistic in their schedules, and unforeseen events happen that rarely speed things up. If a project is behind, the technology support staff member in charge should say so in the report for the first week that she knows about the delay. The project manager should also say what resources would get the project back on schedule. Granted, these resources may not be available, but at least she asked.

Early notification to senior management of schedule slippages is critical. There is nothing worse than having everyone think a project is still on schedule when, in fact, the person responsible knows that it is not.

PROJECT POSTMORTEM

At the end of each project a postmortem should be conducted. This is a meeting between the technology's internal users and the technology support staff in which the project is discussed with all the vision of hindsight. The questions to be asked include:

> What went right?
>
> What went wrong?
>
> What did we learn so we can do better next time?
>
> How could we have anticipated such-and-such delay?

This postmortem, along with the original project narrative and the weekly status reports, make up the history of the project and should be preserved together in a folder or notebook. As time goes by there will begin to be quite a collection of these project notebooks. The notebooks will be invaluable tools to assist the staff in future project planning and in capturing the data on how long certain types of implementation activities typically take. The project notebooks also become the library's documentation on why certain decisions were made in the past.

Step 9.5
Capture and Use Trigger Points
for Assessment of Later Implementations

No matter how well you have planned, your project implementation will take unexpected twists and turns. These will not occur because you didn't plan well, but simply because the world of technology continued to move forward while you were gathering your resources and beginning your implementation. You need to build allowances for this into your implementation plan, especially if your plan covers multiple phases over multiple years.

When you have to make adjustments to your technology plan, it will help if you can review the critical assumptions that led to making the decision under review and determine if those assumptions are still true. For example, you may have decided over the course of several years to replace all of the floppy disk drives in your PCs with CD or DVD rewriters to accommodate your customers' need to output data. But by the time you are ready to actually make the purchase, interest in CD and DVD output may have waned because most of your customers are carrying USB flash drives. If you become so focused on accomplishing each stage of your implementation plan that you don't review the underlying assumptions behind the activities, you may find yourself buying outdated technology or making decisions based on unwarranted financial restrictions.

To ensure that the assumptions are reviewed at the appropriate times, the project manager should identify these decision confirmation points, or "trigger points," in the implementation plan before the implementation begins. Link each trigger point to a specific stage in a multiyear implementation plan. Use Workform 14, Trigger Point Assumptions, to record them. The project manager will want to work with the planning committee chair to list the assumptions for each trigger point now, while he or she can still remember them from the planning process. This will ensure that you remember to validate your assumptions as you proceed through your implementation. (See figure 30.)

FIGURE 30
Example of Workform 14: Trigger Point Assumptions

Project: Upgrading Celeron PCs from Windows 2000 to Windows XP

Stage/Step: Purchasing OS licenses

Trigger Point Decision: Decide if it would be better to replace Celerons rather than upgrading them

Assumptions:

1.   Current Celerons are fast enough to support public access software

2.   Current Celerons support enough RAM for needed public-access applications

---

NOTES

1. "Duration" is elapsed time. It includes both the actual work hours and all the wait time in a project.
2. More about the project prioritization committee can be found in chapter 6.

Chapter 6

Sustain

MILESTONES

By the time you finish this chapter you will know how to

- integrate technology planning into your ongoing operations
- maintain the inventories of hardware, software, networks, and skills

If you have followed the *Technology for Results* process to this point, you have a technology plan in place linked to your service objectives. You have informed the staff and other interested audiences about that plan. Implementation on the first projects is likely to be under way. And you are probably ready to move on to something else, anything else, as long as it's not another round of technology discussions!

The strong temptation in any organization at this point is to declare "mission accomplished" and be done with technology planning for a while. But building your technology infrastructure is a lot like building your materials collection; it is a continuous process of monitoring what is available, selecting those things that meet your service objectives, making them available for use, weeding them out when they are no longer in good condition or being used, and replacing them appropriately with materials (or technology tools) that meet the changing needs and interests of your customers. Would you make your collection development decisions once every two or three years and then move on to other tasks? Of course not, and you shouldn't make your technology decisions that way either.

TASK 10: SUSTAIN THE PLANNING PROCESS

Measuring results is an important piece of the planning process. Regular, ongoing measurement lets you monitor the results of your plans. Usage well beyond your projections may indicate a need for project expansion sooner rather than later. Lower-than-expected results may indicate that more training or publicity is required. Continued low results after attempted corrections may be an indication that the project needs to be phased out and the resources devoted elsewhere.

Step 10.1
Measure and Report Results

Every technology project you implement represents an investment of scarce resources: staff time and money. Nearly every project also has an ongoing component of support (time and money) required to keep it operational. To determine if the ongoing costs are warranted, you need to evaluate the results you have achieved.

As part of the implementation planning, the project manager and project sponsor gave some thought to what could be measured and how that data might be captured. Now someone needs to look at this data, make some judgments about it, and report the results to administration and staff. For each of the projects implemented, ask the following questions.

> What usage is the technology getting? How many units of service are we delivering? How many people are we serving? Are the users reporting satisfaction with the service?

> Is the target audience using the technology we implemented? If not, who *is* using it? Do we need to make changes in the project to make it more attractive to the intended audience? Or is the actual audience a different but equally appropriate set of users? Technology implementations are rife with unexpected consequences. No one accurately predicted the change in the library's user population that resulted from the earliest introduction of Internet workstations. But were those businesspeople and teenagers a bad result? No, it was quite wonderful to see populations we hadn't been reaching before come into the library. Of course, those early Internet workstations brought their share of challenges as well, but in most communities the benefits far outweighed the challenges.

> Were the planning committee's projections of project costs reasonably accurate? Are we realizing the savings we expected from efficiency projects? You can probably estimate the final project cost figures from data in the

project notebook. You particularly need to ask and answer these questions for the cost-efficiency projects you have implemented. The planning process projected a certain expectation of return on investment. If you are not achieving those results, you need to make some changes.

Are you on target or do you need to make changes in the project to improve your results? If changes are needed, what might they be?

Who should be asking and answering these questions? The departments or functions within the library that are using the technologies can be charged with the responsibility of capturing and reporting the data. But if the results indicate that changes are needed, those changes need to be rolled back into the overall technology plan. The chances are pretty good that any needed changes will involve the technology support staff, and their available time has already been allocated to the priorities in the adopted technology plan.

Priorities do need to be changed sometimes. However, changing them should not be done lightly. A project plan and its priorities are like a contract between senior management and the technology support staff. The technology support staff agree to do their best to meet the schedules in the plan and to notify senior management when things are not going according to plan. Senior management agrees to not change the plan and priorities except for the most urgent of reasons.

Having to lay a project aside and come back to it later should be avoided whenever possible. It will take the staff some time to get back up to speed on the project and the total time expended will be greater. When it is necessary to change the priorities and this involves stopping an ongoing project, the decision to do so should come from the highest levels and only after careful consideration.

One way to avoid changes in long-term plans is to not make them. Rather than setting a couple of years' worth of priorities, the library staff can approach technology planning as a recurring process in which priorities are set as resources become available to implement them.

PROJECT PRIORITIZATION COMMITTEE

Instead of creating a plan every two or three years, consider convening a standing committee to regularly review suggestions for new technologies as they become available. This oversight group, the project prioritization committee, functions as a contact point between the technology support staff and the rest of the organization. The committee receives suggestions from the staff, reviews the status of ongoing projects with the technology support staff, and recommends projects to be undertaken as staff resources become available. Members of the committee should represent all of the functional areas within the library.

For new projects, devise a process that encourages any staff member to suggest a potential technology project. If staff know their suggestions will be considered, then you have greatly expanded the number of people in your organization who will monitor ongoing changes in technology. Consider using a form like Workform 15, Technology Suggestion Form, for staff to make their suggestions. This will cause staff to think through the benefits of the suggestions they are submitting and give the committee enough data to make a first cut of proposed projects. Even so, you are still likely to receive more good project suggestions than can be done within the constraints of your staff and budget.

For projects that make the first cut, the committee will ask the technology support staff to make an initial estimate of the staff hours required for each project. This is where the information in the project notebooks becomes valuable. Previous experience with similar projects is the best predictor of needed resources. As the technology support staff gains more experience, the process of projecting requirements will be both easier and more accurate. Even if you have turnover in your technology support staff, you still have the captured experience of earlier projects for new staff to draw on.

The total hours required for new projects or changes to existing projects will most likely exceed the hours available. It is the responsibility of the project prioritization committee to recommend to senior management the ranked priority of the projects. This should be done in consultation with technology support staff, since there may be inter-relationships between the projects.

The committee's recommendations and priorities should be based on the same criteria filters the planning committee applied:

- necessary to continue current critical services
- required by law
- politically advantageous
- progress toward achieving the highest-priority service objectives
- reduces cost or reduces potential cost increases
- the right thing to do

Once senior staff approve the rankings, projects can be assigned and begun as resources become available.

Each time the committee meets, typically quarterly, the list of prioritized projects that have not yet been implemented are thrown back into the consideration pool along with newly suggested projects and any needed changes that have been identified since the last meeting. A single prioritized list results from the deliberations. Once a project is begun, it is seen through to the end.

A standing project prioritization committee also provides a forum for considering the results of pilot projects and determining if a full-blown implementation is desirable. If the committee notices a trend in suggested projects that require skills the technology support staff don't have, then it can highlight the need to either hire the new skills or arrange for training of existing staff.

Step 10.2
Update the Infrastructure Inventory

If your library didn't have a complete inventory of hardware, software, networks, and skills when the technology planning project began, you created one as you went through the planning process. It will be far easier to maintain those inventories on a regular basis than it will be to go through another massive data-gathering effort the next time you need the information.

HARDWARE, SOFTWARE, NETWORKS

Each time you add new equipment in the library or change your wide area network, the technology support staff should add it to the inventory list. Make the inventory entry a step in the installation process. The best time to capture the technical information on a workstation or server is when you have the packing list in your hand because most of the data you need appear on that list. If you discard equipment, remove it from the inventory when you remove it from the building.

Do the same with each new piece of software or each new release you load for existing software. As a step in the loading process, update the inventory. If you permit staff to load software on their own PCs, make it their obligation to let the technology support staff know what they load.

STAFF SKILLS

Maintain the inventory of staff skills as well. Work with your human resources department or training staff to ensure that someone is keeping up with the training each staff member receives. If the core technical skills are not yet a part of each job description, find out how to make that happen in your organization. Talk with human resources and library administration about including a "skills to be acquired in the next rating period" section in each staff member's annual review. This will keep everyone focused on the fact that skills development is a continuous requirement, not a onetime activity.

Step 10.3
Update the Services Inventory

The services inventory you created using Workform 3 in Step 3.2 is another inventory you will want to keep up-to-date. The project prioritization committee can be placed in charge of this inventory. As their recommended projects are implemented, the committee chair should add the new services to the list. The list will be a useful tool for the committee as it prioritizes suggested projects, giving committee members a quick overview of the services already in place in the library.

Continue to Build on Your Success

With a complete inventory of the technologies you are using today, a clear understanding of the services and staff functions those technologies are supporting, and a staff who are encouraged to keep searching for better ways to get the job done, you are well on your way to mastering the challenges of technology planning. It doesn't have to be a major project; it can simply be a regular part of your operational year.

Reviewing your technology plan on a quarterly basis will ensure that you are aware of new technologies as they begin to emerge. You can monitor the growth of public interest and acceptance and be ready to move forward when you determine it is time. With a list of prioritized projects, you will be well positioned to respond to funding opportunities whenever they arise. You will be able to answer questions about why the library did or didn't choose to use a particular technology. You will be able to identify the skills you need on staff to successfully use and manage your technologies. Technology will truly become a tool you use in delivering services, not an extra set of challenges you have to grapple with once every three years.

APPENDIX A

Identifying Technology Options

Whatever the difficulties librarians may have in keeping up with current technologies and developing trends, lack of information is not among them. We are all surrounded by vast amounts of information about technology in the popular press, in library literature, on television, and through the Internet itself. As a matter of fact, there is so much information available that it is often difficult to find what you need. At one time or another you have probably felt like the woman who typed a request into an Internet search engine and got 12,350 hits. She didn't want 12,350 hits—she wanted the one right answer!

How Can You Know What Options Exist?

While there may be no such thing as "one right answer" to your technology needs, there are a number of ways that you can discover information about technology-based services in use today, as well as identify and track future trends. Most of the traditional forms of information sharing—including reading library and technology journals and books; talking to other librarians, information professionals, and technology experts; and attending conference programs—work well for learning about new technologies and how libraries are using them. Electronic forums for exchanging news and experiences also exist; these include discussion lists, blogs, digital communities, and general exploring on the Internet.

Look Online

One of the earliest electronic communication techniques to be widely used in libraries was membership mailing lists or electronic discussion lists. These lists are essentially electronic conversations. They work like e-mail, but instead of sending your message to one recipient you send it to all of the subscribers to the list. The recipients can then respond to you directly or to the entire list. There are hundreds of electronic discussion groups on every aspect of technology and on every aspect of public libraries as well. PUBLIB is the oldest and most popular national discussion list for public librarians, and it regularly addresses a broad range of public library issues, including those surrounding technology. Most states also have statewide library discussion lists that address similar topics. There are also lists for librarians interested in discussing specialized areas of technology, for example, Web4Lib and XML4Lib.

Digital communities are another way to talk with others. The best-known library-oriented digital community is WebJunction, which bills itself as "an online community where library staff meet to share ideas, solve problems, take online courses—and have fun."[1] WebJunction is a library-focused "portal," i.e., a website that offers a broad array of resources and services. Funded initially by a grant from the Bill and Melinda Gates Library Foundation, WebJunction is now hosted by OCLC. It exists to support the sharing of knowledge and experience among library staff and to provide the broadest public access to information technology. In addition to providing message boards where members can ask questions or contribute answers, WebJunction offers a large array of reports on funding and managing technology, and it links to websites offering assistance in areas ranging from product reviews to technology planning.

Weblogs or blogs are growing rapidly as sources of information on the Internet. According to Steven Cohen in his book *Keeping Current: Advanced Internet Strategies to Meet Librarian and Patron Needs,* a blog is a "chronological listing of postings to a web site with links to other web sites, news articles, or anything else that the writers find interesting on the Web."[2] Librarians are using blogs both to communicate with their customers and to communicate with each other. The Weblogs Compendium (http://www.lights.com/weblogs/index.html) includes lists of library-oriented blogs on a wide variety of topics created by librarians from around the world. The Shifted Librarian (http:// www.theshiftedlibrarian.com/) and TechnoBiblio, "Where Librarians and TechnoGeeks Speak the Same Language" (http://www.technobiblio.com/), are just two examples of relevant blogs. Some blogs let their readers comment and post to the site, which makes them another way to talk to other librarians interested in the same issues you are.

The Internet in general contains an astonishing treasure trove of information. If you want to know something about any aspect of technology, the chances are excellent you can find it somewhere in cyberspace. There are a number of regularly published journals that will keep you up-to-date with the latest technology news; some are electronic only, others are electronic versions of print journals. Some are specifically library technology oriented. The Public Library Association hosts *Tech Notes* (http://www.ala.org/ala/pla/plapubs/technotes/technotes.htm), which offers "short, Web-based papers introducing specific technologies for public librarians." Library Technology Guides (http://www.library technology.org/) is a website that "aims to provide comprehensive and objective information related to the field of library automation." *Library Journal*'s "InfoTech" column is available electronically at www.libraryjournal.com. *Current Cites* (http://sunsite.berkeley.edu/CurrentCites/) is a monthly publication produced by a team of librarians who monitor information technology literature in both print and digital forms and selectively annotate useful sources. The Dynix Institute (http://www.dynix.com/institute/) offers a series of web-based seminars on a variety of topics, including promoting online collection use, introductions to new technologies, and leadership skills in technology-enabled libraries. All of the seminars are archived on the Web and are available for replay on demand.

Infopeople, whose primary role is "to provide broad-based technology-related training for those working in California libraries," archives its training webcasts at http://www .infopeople.org/training/webcasts/archived.html and makes them available to librarians outside of California after they are broadcast.

You can also use one or more of the Internet search engines to find the information you need. Most library reference staff are excellent search engine users and can guide you to finding something on the Internet on almost any topic. Alternatively, Infopeople's Best Search Tools Chart (http://infopeople.org/search/chart.html) provides a very clear overview of the various search engines, and their Best Search Engines Quick Guide (http:// infopeople.org/search/guide.html) offers some useful preliminary searching hints.

Read

Many librarians are still more comfortable learning from the printed word than the computer screen. Fortunately, there are hundreds of print resources available on all aspects of technology, including adaptive technology for people with disabilities. Magazines and journals usually provide the best information on current issues and topics. Public library professionals should certainly read major library publications such as *Library Journal, American Libraries*, and *Public Libraries*, all of which routinely carry stories and news bulletins about library technology issues. Journals that deal specifically with library technology include *Smart Libraries, Library Hi-Tech, Computers in Libraries, Library Technology Reports*, and *Information Technology and Libraries*. There are also journals that deal with electronic databases and reference tools, such as *Information Today, Online*, and *Searcher*. Finally, there are journals like *Library Trends* that explore the future of libraries, including the impact of technology.

In addition, there are dozens of technology magazines, many of them with a very narrow focus. There are magazines devoted to Microsoft Windows, interesting World Wide Web sites, computer gaming, portable computing, Macintosh computers, and PCs. Issues in developing and managing networks are covered in *Network, LAN Times*, and *InfoWorld*, all of which have electronic editions on the Internet as well as print versions. In fact, it is likely that you can find a magazine about almost any aspect of computing that interests you. The Internet search engine Yahoo provides an index to many of these technology magazines.[3] There are also a number of more general technology magazines, such as *Wired*, which provide an overview of technology issues, identify trends, and help readers to understand how various technologies interrelate. Finally, there are mainstream magazines, from *Business Week* to *People*, which regularly include information about how current technologies are affecting people's lives. Because they are written for the layperson and often include a context for the information they provide, these articles can be very helpful in getting a sense of the bigger picture.

Books can provide a more in-depth look at technology. Check out any bookstore and you will find aisles of new books on all aspects of technology, from scholarly tomes on the impact of technology on society to specific how-to manuals for popular software programs. There are titles devoted to adaptive technology for people with disabilities, as well as titles focused on adaptive technology in libraries. Your library collection probably already includes the best of these resources. In addition to these general books, there are reports from specific studies that have looked at the impact of technology on our world and that contain valuable information for librarians. You will find citations in the library journals noted above to new and important reports as they are published. One publisher of these types of reports is the Pew Trust (http://www.pewinternet.org/index.asp).

Talk

Librarians are among the most helpful people around and they are used to answering questions. After all, that is what they do for a living. In your search for current information and your attempt to identify future trends, you will probably find that your colleagues are extremely helpful. As you think about your colleagues, don't be parochial. Libraries of all types are incorporating a wide range of technologies into their ongoing operations. Your local school librarians, local college librarians, and even staff from libraries that are not as technologically advanced as your own may have things to teach you.

You don't have to limit your conversations to other librarians. No matter how small your community is, you will find that there are technical experts available to you locally. Make friends with your city or county information systems staff. They make, and will continue to make, decisions that will affect library operations. They can be a wonderful source of information about the big picture, and the more they know about your library and its technology needs, the more likely they are to make decisions that will be advantageous to you. Local computer user groups can be another source of information and assistance. If you are planning to provide public access to the Internet, you may want to get these people involved to help provide assistance to the public. They may also be able to give you information about expected product enhancements, as well as tips and tools for using products more effectively.

Last but not least, there are sales and vendor representatives from library automation firms. Naturally, they will present their information in the context of their own products. However, most vendor representatives are very knowledgeable about the field of library automation and can provide you with excellent insights into what the near future might bring.

Attend Programs at Meetings and Conferences

Library associations at the local, state, regional, and national levels all present regular conferences with programs designed to keep working librarians informed about all aspects of the profession. Your local and state conferences probably include panels of working librarians talking about how they have addressed technology problems that you may be currently facing. These conferences often feature a nationally recognized automation expert to provide an overview of the current technology along with forecasts about the future. Regional and national conferences also include panels of working librarians, but rather than speaking from the perspective of a single state, these panelists provide a mix of ideas from around the country. These larger conferences normally feature more technology experts as well. For example, if you attend the American Library Association's Annual Conference, held in late June each year, you will have the opportunity to hear many of the leaders in library automation as well as technology experts from other fields. The Public Library Association's National Conference, held every two years in the spring, focuses on programs of specific interest to public librarians and always features discussions of the latest technologies and their impact on public libraries. The Library Information and Technology Association also periodically presents national conferences and regional institutes that are focused solely on the technology affecting libraries. Other specialty professional conferences include the annual National Online Meeting and the Internet Librarian conference. The Information Today website (http://www.infotoday .com/conferences.shtml) includes a list of conferences aimed at information professionals.

Your conference attendance does not have to be restricted to library-specific conferences. There are thousands of technology conferences held around the world each year. The TradeShow Plaza (http://www.tradeshowplaza.com) provides a complete listing of these conferences by subject or location. You might want to check out the conferences in your area to see if any of them include topics that will affect your library.

NOTES

1. Available at http://www.webjunction.org/.
2. Steven M. Cohen, *Keeping Current: Advanced Internet Strategies to Meet Librarian and Patron Needs* (Chicago: American Library Association, 2003), 49.
3. Available at http://dir.yahoo.com/Computers_and_Internet/News_and_Media/Magazines/.

APPENDIX B

Developing a Technical Inventory

There are many ways to gather and organize information about the technical aspects of your current environment. Some libraries keep databases or spreadsheets with the technical descriptions of equipment, lists of installed software, and network diagrams developed and maintained by their technology support staff. Libraries with a limited number of devices may capture the information on written forms in a notebook. Members of consortia may find that their consortium support staff keep an inventory of the equipment and software in each member library and network diagrams for the entire consortium.

If you don't have an existing inventory of installed equipment and software to work with, then you will need to conduct a physical inventory. Depending on the size of your library and the extent to which you are already supporting technology-based services, this series of steps may be either simple or somewhat complex to complete. If your library is a member of a consortium that provides most of the services you use, the inventory of your local environment may only require you to know about the PCs in your building and to call your consortium technical support staff to ask a few questions. If your library has a number of branches or a large number of technology services, assessing the current environment will take some time and effort to complete.

Hardware and Software

Begin by asking the technology support staff, or the technology staff representative on the planning committee, to complete Workform 16, Technical Inventory, for all of the servers in your computer room. Then move on to counting the number of PCs you have in each facility. Finally, count the number of other direct public service or staff devices you have in each location. Don't forget to count any devices that are in the location but aren't being used. These may represent resources you could be using, or they may be devices that have outlived their usefulness and need to be discarded.

What Information Do You Need?

For PC workstations and servers, the basic technical information you require at a minimum includes

- location in the library
- name of the device
- type and speed of processor
- available memory (RAM)
- disk space, total and available
- operating system
- network connection, if any

For each workstation or server you will also want a list of the software installed on the machine, including desktop security and virus protection information. Additional data beyond the basics you might want to collect for each machine to create a complete inventory include

- manufacturer and model number
- serial number
- removable media (floppy drives, CD or DVD readers and writers)
- any devices the equipment is responsible for sharing over the network (disk, printer, fax modem, scanner, backup device, etc.)

For peripheral devices such as printers and scanners, at a minimum you need to know

- name of the device
- location in the library
- network connection, if any

Where Can You Get the Information?

Fortunately, technical tools exist to help with this task. Most PC desktops (Apples included; "PC" is used here as a generic term, not meant to indicate only a Windows/Intel machine) and servers have a function that allows you to view system information, including most of the basic information outlined above. Once you have displayed the information, you can write it on a data collection form such as Workform 16, or enter it into a database or spreadsheet if you have the technical skills to use these programs.

TechSurveyor, a technology asset tracking tool designed for nonprofit organizations by NPower, offers an automated way to compile a complete technical inventory of your hardware, software, peripherals, and networks, as well as the technology skills of your staff.[1] The TechSurveyor website offers a downloadable inventory tool that will create an assessment of each workstation and server. Most of the workstation and server data listed above are captured, including information on the software available on each device. Information on peripherals may be entered by library staff at the TechSurveyor site to create a full inventory of equipment. Data may be stored at TechSurveyor or downloaded to your own spreadsheet.

Networks

Almost all automated library services rely on some kind of network to operate. Therefore, every public library probably has some type of network in place today. Networks make it possible for computers to communicate with each other. Local area networks (LANs) are generally confined to a single building or group of buildings. Wide area networks (WANs) connect computers over larger distances, usually over public or private telecommunications lines such as telephone circuits or cable television systems. The Internet is the world's largest wide area network.

What Information Do You Need?

The key information you need about the library's network is its bandwidth, which is the amount of data that a network can carry in a fixed amount of time. Bandwidth is reported in "bits per second." The bandwidth of a library's networks is crucial because most of the technology-based services a library offers involve moving data over the library's networks: between workstations and the library's own servers (web pages or integrated library system data), between Internet resources and the library's workstations, or between the library's servers and people on the Internet. If you don't have enough bandwidth for the data being moved, delays in retrieving and displaying data (poor response time) result.

Wide area networks vary widely in bandwidth. A dial-up telephone connection to the Internet usually supports somewhere between 26,000 and 52,000 bits per second (26 and 52 Kbps). Many of the earliest dedicated phone lines installed by libraries were 56 Kbps lines, and in some rural areas these may still be the only line speeds available at a reasonable cost. E-rate funding has enabled many libraries to upgrade from 56 Kbps to higher bandwidths. As this is being written, a common bandwidth in most areas is T1 or 1.544 Mbps (i.e., 1,544,000 bits per second). Cable connections offer a wide range of bandwidths and newer telephone company services support a range of bandwidths between 56 Kbps and T1. Bandwidths higher than T1 are available for libraries that require them and can afford them.

The bandwidth of a local area network is much higher than that of WANs. In local area networks, the most common bandwidths between desktop devices are 10 million bits per second (10Mbps) and 100 million bits per second (100 Mbps). Even the lowest of these speeds is six times faster than a T1 WAN connection. LAN bandwidth is rarely a problem for most libraries.

The lowest bandwidth between two computers is the one which will affect the response time. If you are moving data between two devices sharing a local area network—between a workstation and a printer, for example—the LAN bandwidth is what matters. If you are moving data between a workstation in a branch and your integrated library system or a web server at your main library, the WAN bandwidth between the two locations will govern the speed. When you are moving data through the Internet, WAN bandwidth between your library and your library's Internet service provider (ISP) is important. And sometimes the bandwidth between your ISP and *their* connection to the Internet is important information as well, particularly if your ISP is a local company, not a regional or national supplier of Internet connectivity.

If you work in a multibranch library, you will want to know what the bandwidth is between each branch and your computer room, where your library's primary servers (integrated library system, web, etc.) are located. Your computer room may be in your main library, an administrative headquarters, at your consortium's headquarters, or in a city or county data center. If you outsource the library's web services to a commercial firm, one of your "computer rooms" is at that location.

You also need to know what the bandwidth is between each location and the Internet. For some libraries, the computer room and the Internet are accessed over the same data connection. In this model, pictured in figure 31, the data connection to the ISP usually runs between the computer room and the ISP; all of the branches share that Internet connection through their own data connections to the computer room. Other libraries may have multiple data connections in a single location, one connecting to the computer room and another connecting to the Internet, often through a local cable company. Figure 32 shows this model. Determine what model describes your library and collect information on all the data connections at each location. Section E of Workform 16 provides a format for recording your findings.

FIGURE 31
Single-Line Internet Connection

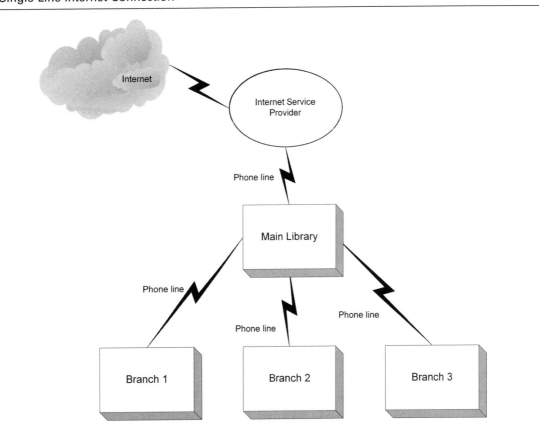

FIGURE 32
Multiline Internet Connections

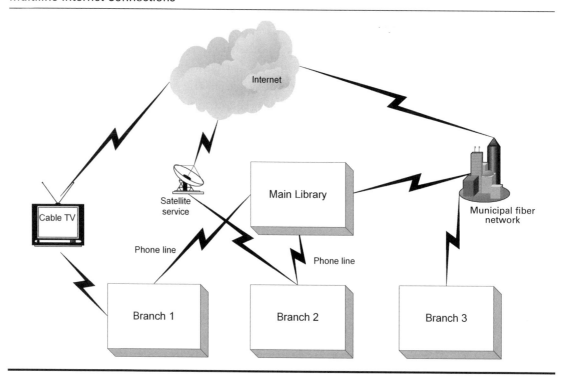

To summarize, you need to gather bandwidth information on each of the following data connections:

- from each library location to your computer room
- from each library location to the Internet
- from your computer room(s) to the Internet
- from your ISP to their own bandwidth supplier

Where Can You Get the Information?

If your library technical staff doesn't already know the answer to how much bandwidth is available at each location, you can ask your bandwidth supplier to provide the information. Typically, the bandwidth supplier is either your telephone or cable television company. In cities and counties with fiber-based government networks, your bandwidth supplier may be another department in your government. Some libraries, especially in rural areas, are using satellites or other wireless technologies for data transmission. Again, you can ask the company or government agency providing the service to give you the data. Some libraries and many consortia use a mix of suppliers, based on what is available and cost effective in a particular geographical area. In some states, basic library bandwidth is provided through the state library and you may need to ask some of your bandwidth questions there.

You also need to ask your bandwidth supplier if your bandwidth is symmetric or asymmetric. "Symmetric bandwidth" means you have the same amount of bandwidth for data traffic going both to and from your locations. "Asymmetric bandwidth" means you have more bandwidth going in one direction than the other. Typically, asymmetric bandwidth means you have more *downstream* (coming into the location) than *upstream* (going out of the location) bandwidth. Higher downstream bandwidth works for most library branch locations; after all, a single mouse click can get you an entire web page of data. But if you are connecting servers to the Internet and it will be your computers delivering that web page, then limited upstream bandwidth won't meet your needs. Your computer room should not be connected to the Internet via an asymmetric service that limits upstream bandwidth.

NOTE

1. TechSurveyor is available at http://techsurveyor.npower.org/techsurveyor/computer_profile.asp.

Appendix C

Groups Reaching Agreement

Issues

Most public libraries make extensive use of committees and teams to explore options, make recommendations about future services, and review and evaluate existing programs. No matter what their purpose, all committees and teams have one thing in common: to be successful their members must be able to reach agreement on the issues under consideration. As anyone who has ever served on a committee knows, this isn't easy. Problems include lack of a clear committee or team charge, groups that are too large or too small, group leaders with poor facilitation skills, group members with competing agendas, lack of accountability, and the absence of official action on committee recommendations. These issues are discussed in more detail in the following sections.

The Charge

Every committee or team should have a clearly stated charge, and every member of the committee should understand that charge. The charge should include

> an explicit description of what the committee is expected to accomplish
>
> the time frame for the committee's deliberations
>
> the person or group that will receive the committee's report
>
> the process that will be used to review and act upon the committee's work
>
> the time frame for that review and action

Source: Sandra Nelson, *The New Planning for Results: A Streamlined Approach* (Chicago: American Library Association, 2001), 235–45.

Group Size

Committees and teams can range in size from two or three people to as many as twenty or thirty people. The decision concerning the size of the group is a trade-off. Smaller committees are usually easier to work with because fewer people are involved. Communication is quicker, orientation takes less time, discussion and consensus may move more quickly, and smaller committees are less expensive to support. However, smaller groups may be open to potential criticism of narrow thinking or elitism. If the workload you envision for committee members is heavy, a small group may be overwhelmed and burn out before the committee completes its work.

Larger committees usually reflect a wider range of interests and can include people with a variety of expertise. Because the interests of the members may be more diverse, a wider scope of issues might be addressed. On the other hand, meetings will require more time for discussion and reaching consensus. Some committee members may feel lost in the crowd and lose enthusiasm. Large groups are also more difficult to lead. If the group is going to have more than twelve members, it is advisable to make arrangements for a trained facilitator to be the leader.

Leadership

Committees and teams are most effective when they are led by people who understand how groups work and have strong facilitation skills. Most library committees and teams are responsible for problem solving or information gathering. In these types of group activities, leaders are responsible for involving all members of the group in the work of the group and ensuring that everyone has a say in the group's decisions. Generally, group members participate more and take a greater level of responsibility for the group's decisions if the leader focuses his or her energies on *facilitating participation* rather than on providing answers. See figure 33: Group Participation Chart, for more information on group leaders.

Membership

A committee or team is only as strong as its members. Group members normally play one of three roles:

Builders. These people are interested in the work of the committee and focus their energies on the successful completion of the group's charge.

Blockers. These people get in the way of the work of the committee by behaving in ways that block progress. There are dozens of behaviors that can derail an effective meeting. See figure 34: Problem Behaviors in Meetings, for more information on blockers.

Maintainers. These people are more interested in maintaining relationships than in the work of the committee. They are the bridge between the builders and the blockers.

Every committee needs builders and maintainers, and unfortunately, almost all committees have at least one blocker. It is the leader's responsibility to see to it that the members of the group, no matter what their primary motivation, work together effectively.

FIGURE 33
Group Participation Chart

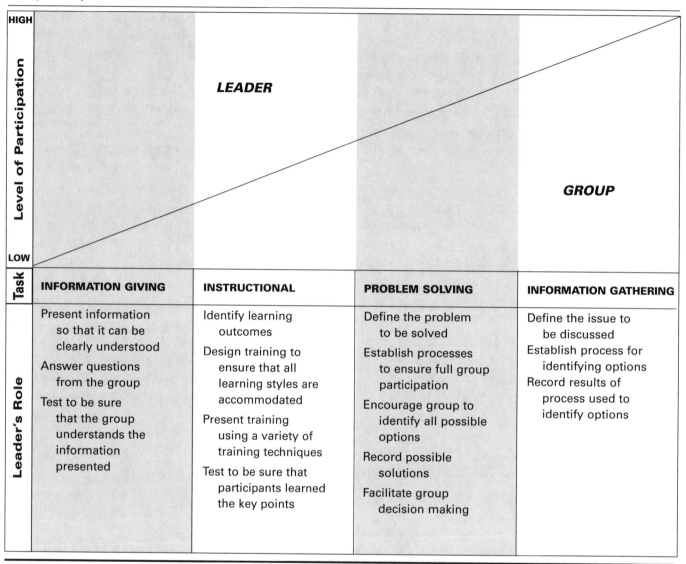

Accountability

Committees and teams should be held accountable for their actions, just as individuals are. All too often the old saying, "when everyone is responsible, no one is responsible" comes into play with committees. It is not only possible but desirable to make it clear to a group that they are collectively responsible for specific results.

Action on Recommendations

If you ask any committee or group member what was the most frustrating thing about the group experience, far too many of them will say that they never saw any results from all of their work. Submitting a group report is often likened to Henry Wadsworth Longfellow's words: "I shot an arrow into the air, it fell to earth, I know not where."

FIGURE 34
Problem Behaviors in Meetings

PROBLEM	BEHAVIOR	SUGGESTED SOLUTION
Latecomer	Always late	Start meetings on time—don't wait for stragglers. Do not recap meeting when Latecomer arrives but offer to provide a recap during the first break.
Early Leaver	Never stays until meeting is adjourned	Set a time for adjournment and get a commitment from all members at the beginning of the meeting to stay until that time.
Clown	Always telling jokes; deflects group from task at hand	Laugh at the joke and then ask the Clown to comment on the topic under discussion. If the Clown responds with another joke, again ask for a comment on the topic.
Broken Record	Brings up same point over and over again	Write the Broken Record's concern on a flip chart and post to provide assurance that the concern has been heard and will be addressed.
Doubting Thomas	Reacts negatively to most ideas	Encourage all group members to wait to make decisions until all points of view have been heard. Let Doubting Thomases express their concerns, but do not let them argue with others who do not share that negativity.
Dropout	Nonparticipant	Try asking Dropout's opinion during meeting or at break. Break group into groups of two or three to encourage everyone to participate.
Whisperer	Members having private conversations	Make eye contact with speakers. Pause briefly until you have their attention and then begin to speak again.
Loudmouth	Must be center of attention; talks constantly	Acknowledge Loudmouths when they begin to talk and let them have their say. Then, if Loudmouths interrupt others, remind them that they have had their say.
Attacker	Makes very critical comments, often directed at leader	Thank Attacker for the observation; ask other group members what they think. If the person's attacks are directed at another group member, the leader has a responsibility to intervene. It is best to resolve these conflicts privately and not in front of the whole group.
Interpreter	Often says "In other words" or "What she really means"	Check this in public with original speaker.
Know-It-All	Always has the answer	Remind the group that all members have expertise; that's the reason for meeting. Ask others to respond to Know-It-All's comments.
Teacher's Pet	Tries to monopolize the leader's attention	Be encouraging, but break eye contact. Get group members to talk to one another. Lessen your omnipotence by reflecting "What do you think?" back to the Teacher's Pet.

Library managers who appoint committees or teams to make recommendations have to establish processes for reviewing and acting on those recommendations. All group members should be aware of the review process and be kept informed of the status of the review from beginning to the point at which a final decision has been made.

Evaluating Methods of Reaching Decisions

Three general approaches to reaching agreement in groups are consensus building, voting, and the forced-choice process. Each of these decision-making approaches can be used effectively to lead the group to a decision. The important thing is matching the approach to the situation. Four measures can be used to help you decide which approach will be most effective for the situation: the importance of the quality of the decision made; the time it takes to make the decision; the level of support the members of the group have for the decision; and the learning that takes place while the members make the decision.

Quality of the Decision

The first measure is the importance of the quality of the decision that is produced. For example, a group that decides very quickly to vote to select priorities may not make as informed a decision as a group that spends the time needed to explore all of the options in detail before making a decision. On the other hand, not all situations are equally critical. Decisions such as where the group will eat lunch or when the next meeting will be held don't require extensive discussion.

Time Required

The second measure is the time it takes to reach the decision. To continue with the preceding example, the group that voted quickly obviously made a decision in less time than the group that explored options more fully. There is often a trade-off between the length of time a group spends on a decision and the quality of the final decision. However, that is not always true: at times groups get stuck in a seemingly endless process of data collection and discussion and never do make any decision—good or bad.

Level of Support

The third measure is the desired level of support the group will have for the decision that has been made. Consensus building, by its very nature, creates the highest level of group support for the decisions being made because everyone has to agree with the decisions before they become final. On the other hand, the forced-choice process, which averages choices made by group members to determine priorities, has the potential for resulting in decisions that none of the group supports wholeheartedly.

Development of Expertise

In some cases, it is important that the group members be given an opportunity to develop expertise in the area under consideration. For instance, if a team is going to be involved in making decisions about technology issues for the library for the next year, it is clearly important that the members of the team become knowledgeable about technology options and stay aware of changes in the field. In other cases, there is no need to support the development of such expertise. A committee of children's librarians who are responsible for developing and presenting a puppet show to publicize the summer reading program will probably have the expertise they need to accomplish their charge.

Methods for Reaching Agreement

Consensus Building

Quality of decision:
Normally very good
Time required:
Time intensive
Group support for decision:
High
Development of expertise:
High

Consensus building is a process by which group members seek a mutually acceptable resolution to the issue under discussion. Note that consensus does not mean that everyone agrees that the solution is the best of all possible answers. A group has reached consensus when everyone can and will support the decision.

WHEN TO USE

This approach is best suited for making important decisions. Consensus promotes hard thinking that really gets at the issues. It can be slow, and it is occasionally painful; however, when a group finally reaches consensus, it has developed a solution that will have the support needed for implementation. Since consensus requires so much energy, the group should agree that the outcome of the decision is worth the effort. Such outcomes might include long-range planning, the development of a new program or service, or the revision of the library's job descriptions. In each of these situations, people probably care deeply about the outcome, and their support will be required to successfully implement the decision.

WHAT TO DO

People reach consensus by talking about issues in a fair and open environment. That means that the group leader will have to ensure that each member of the group has an opportunity to be heard, that no idea is discarded without a thorough review and discussion, and that all members of the group take responsibility for finding a mutually agreeable decision.

The national best seller *Getting to Yes: Negotiating Agreement without Giving In* identifies four steps to reaching consensus.[1]

1. *Separate people from the problem.*

   People often feel strongly about issues under discussion, and discussions can shift quickly from issues to personalities. It is important to keep the discussion firmly focused on the problem under review.

2. *Focus on interests, not positions.*

   Positions are the opinions that each group member brings to the discussion before the discussion begins. These positions get in the way of reaching consensus because they tend to be "all or nothing." To reach consensus, group members will have to focus on the problem and their mutual interest in resolving it and not on their preconceived positions.

3. *Generate a variety of options before deciding what to do.*

   There is no one right way to do anything. Consensus building involves identifying and discussing all of the ways the problem might be resolved. This is surprisingly difficult. Most people see problem solving as narrowing the options, not expanding them.

4. *Base decisions on objective criteria.*

   This is a critical step in the consensus-building process. The group members must be able to define the criteria they will use to evaluate the options they have identified. If they can't agree on criteria, the group members are likely to revert to their positions when reviewing the options.

Voting

Quality of decision:
Varies
Time required:
Low to moderate
Group support for decision:
Moderate
Development of expertise:
Low to moderate

When people think about group decision-making processes, the first process that comes to mind is voting. Our whole society is based on the premise that the majority rules. We have all been voting on things since we were children. Voting is democratic, it's generally fair, and it's always quick and easy. However, there are some potential problems with voting. It can short-circuit consideration of all of the options, and if the issue is particularly contentious, it can split the group into winners and losers.

WHEN TO USE

If the decision under discussion is not critical and not worth a lot of discussion, it may be easiest to vote with a simple hand count. It is perfectly acceptable to take a hand count to decide where the group will have lunch. Hand counts can be used to make procedural decisions (how long the meetings will last, when the next meeting will be held, etc.).

If the decision is important, the dot exercise voting process is more flexible and allows group members to express their opinions in more detail. It also provides a visual summary of the group members' preferred choices. The dot exercise might be used to identify activities that would help the library achieve the goals and objectives in the long-range plan or identify topics for a staff-day program.

WHAT TO DO: DOT EXERCISE

The basic dot exercise process is quite straightforward. The process allows a large number of people to vote on a variety of options in a short period of time.

1. The leader first lists all the options on newsprint with enough space next to or between the items to allow committee members to place adhesive dots.
2. Each participant is given five self-adhesive colored dots.
3. The group members vote by putting dots on the flip chart sheets next to their choices. Members may vote for five separate items, or they may load their vote, or "bullet vote," by giving an item more than one dot.

4. Count the votes by totaling the number of dots by each item.

5. Share and discuss the outcome of the voting exercise. Does the outcome seem to reflect the earlier discussions? Are clear priorities and consensus emerging? Ask those who voted for items under discussion that received few votes to talk about their reasons for selecting those items under discussion.

A variation on the basic dot exercise helps to balance the effect of "bullet voting," which occurs when members place more than one of their dots by a single option. If the group is large, the bullet votes of one or two people will not have much impact, but if the group is small, those one or two people can essentially set priorities for the entire committee. With a small group you might consider avoiding the impact of bullet voting by asking that committee members use a star to indicate their top priority. Then count votes by totaling the number of dots by each item and the number of stars by each item. Next, they share and discuss the outcome of the voting exercise. What is the difference, if any, between the priorities reflected by the dots and the stars? Does the outcome seem to reflect the earlier discussions? Are clear priorities and consensus emerging?

Forced Choice

> *Quality of decision:*
>   Varies
> *Time required:*
>   Low
> *Group support for decision:*
>   Low to moderate
> *Development of expertise:*
>   Low

Most people find it virtually impossible to compare the relative merits of more than three or four items. This process allows people to compare any number of items, each against the other, to determine which are the most important.

WHEN TO USE

The forced-choice process is an effective way of helping groups that have become mired in discussion to look at the options under review in a different way. The process does just what its name says: it forces people to make decisions from among a number of competing possibilities. The process also provides the information needed to place the options in priority order, based on the average ranking by each group member. That, however, is also the main weakness in the process. Because the priority of the options is determined by averaging, it is quite possible that the final list will not reflect the opinions of any single individual in the group. However, the process does identify items with little support. These can be excluded from the discussion, and one of the processes discussed in this chapter can be used to allow the group to move forward to reach final agreement on the remaining options.

WHAT TO DO

1. List the options under review and number each. It is easier for the group members to vote if each of them has a copy of the options.

2. Prepare a forced-choice workform (see figure 35: Sample Forced-Choice Workform, for an example) and make a copy for each group member. The worksheet in figure 35 can be used to prioritize up to ten items. If you are working with more than ten items, you will need to modify the workform to allow for the extra choices.

3. Each of the group members will complete the forced-choice process. (See figure 35 for directions.)

FIGURE 35

Sample Forced-Choice Workform

Assign a number to each of the activities you are prioritizing. This worksheet will help you evaluate up to 10 items against every other item, each time determining which of your choices is more important. Begin in Column A. Compare the first and second items and circle the number of the one you think is more important (1 or 2). Continuing in Column A, compare the first item and the third item, again circling the activity you think is more important (1 or 3). Continue through all of the columns.

A	B	C	D	E	F	G	H	I
1 2								
1 3	2 3							
1 4	2 4	3 4						
1 5	2 5	3 5	4 5					
1 6	2 6	3 6	4 6	5 6				
1 7	2 7	3 7	4 7	5 7	6 7			
1 8	2 8	3 8	4 8	5 8	6 8	7 8		
1 9	2 9	3 9	4 9	5 9	6 9	7 9	8 9	
1 10	2 10	3 10	4 10	5 10	6 10	7 10	8 10	9 10

To score your ratings, add the number of times you circled each number and place the total by the appropriate number below. Note that you must add vertically and horizontally to be sure that you include all circled choices. The item with the highest number is the one you think is most important.

1= ____ 2= ____ 3= ____ 4= ____ 5= ____ 6= ____ 7= ____ 8= ____ 9= ____ 10= ____

4. After each group member totals the number of times each option was circled, the option with the highest total is the one with the highest priority for that person.

5. The leader will help the group see how the group members' selections compare with one another. This may be done in one of two ways:

> Total the points for each choice from all of the group members. The choice with the highest total score is the most important; the next is the second most important, etc.

> Determine where each of the group members ranked each option by asking how many ranked a given option as the highest priority, how many ranked it as the second highest priority, etc. In this case, the option with the highest average ranking becomes the highest priority.

NOTE

1. Roger Fisher and William Ury, and for the Second Edition, Bruce Patton, *Getting to Yes: Negotiating Agreement without Giving In,* 2d ed. (New York: Penguin Books, 1991), 10–11.

Appendix D

Groups Identifying Options

Issues

Library managers must make decisions every day. Sometimes they make those decisions alone; sometimes they give the responsibility for making a decision to a committee or task force. In either case, the first step in any decision-making process is to identify the options to be considered. Regardless of whether the ultimate decision will be made by a single person or a group, it is usually more effective to involve a number of people in the process of identifying options. The greater number of viable options decision makers have to consider, the more likely they are to make effective decisions.

At first glance, it would seem that identifying options would be fairly easy. After all, almost everyone seems to have opinions about almost everything. In reality, when you begin to work with groups to help them identify options, you discover that people's preconceived ideas make it more difficult, not easier, to identify a range of options. Other problems include the tendency to think that there is only one right answer to every question, the difficulty in identifying new options for old problems, the dominance of the group by one or more members, and the effect of peer pressure on group activities that results in a tendency among group members to minimize the appearance of conflict. Finally, it is important to remember the old computer acronym GIGO (garbage in—garbage out). It applies here, too. You have to have the right people involved in the process to identify effective options. The right people, in this instance, include people with some understanding of the problem and some experience or knowledge that provides them with a basis for suggesting solutions. Each of these issues is discussed in greater detail in the following sections.

Source: Sandra Nelson, *The New Planning for Results: A Streamlined Approach* (Chicago: American Library Association, 2001), 223–34.

Searching for the One Right Answer

It is important for the group leader to lay the groundwork carefully for the process to be used to identify options, stressing the need to look at a variety of points of view. Many people are uncomfortable with ambiguity and find the concept of multiple, valid options difficult to understand. Instead they search for the absolute answer to any question. They are inclined to make premature decisions to avoid having to deal with uncomfortable choices. Most groups need periodic reminders that the purpose of this part of the decision-making process is to identify as many options as possible and that even ideas that seem wildly unrealistic at first glance may lead to new insights or choices.

Thinking "Inside the Box"

In general, the more familiar people are with a situation, the more difficult they find it to consider the situation objectively or creatively. This can be a particular problem in libraries because so many staff members have worked in the same system for decades. The group leader will want to encourage people to look with new eyes at the issues under consideration. This might be done in at least three ways.

Move from the specific to the general. Encourage group members to broaden their frames of reference. For instance, instead of thinking about the public library as an institution, broaden the definition to include all libraries, and then broaden it again to include all information providers. Remind the participants of the story of the railroad company executives who defined their business as "railroading." Not much later the competition from trucking and airfreight had pushed them close to bankruptcy. If the executives had understood that they were in the transportation business and not just the railroad business, the executives might well have been able to identify alternative options.

Look at what is happening beyond our own field. We can learn a lot from other organizations, both profit and not-for-profit. For instance, many library managers have benefited from management books written by such authors as Stephen Covey and Peter Drucker even though their books were intended primarily for businesspeople. The United Way has been very involved in helping not-for-profit organizations define the results of the services they provide, and the United Way manual *Measuring Program Outcomes: A Practical Approach* would be a valuable tool for any library manager.[1]

Question everything. James Thurber once said, "It is better to ask some of the questions than know all of the answers." When someone says, "We've always done it this way," ask "Why?" When someone says, "We can't do that" ask "Why not?" Why can't we provide off-site access to information? Why can't we let users access their e-mail accounts on library equipment? Why can't we use e-book technology to deliver current materials more quickly and cost effectively? Why can't we use wireless technology? Why can't we collaborate with another organization to provide a service?

Dealing with Dominant Behaviors

Every group has one or more dominant members. The source of their dominance varies: some people control a group by sheer force of personality. Others are dominant because of their positions. Yet others use their expertise (real or perceived) to control a group. Finally, some people dominate groups because they are bullies and attack anyone who disagrees with them or tries to express an alternative point of view.

It is critical for the group leader to make it clear to all group members that each person's opinion is important. This message may have to be repeated several times during the process. Then the group leader must control the behavior of the dominant members in the group. This can be done by waiting until others have spoken before asking the dominant members for their opinions. Another possibility is to divide the group into smaller subgroups, which has the effect of minimizing the impact of the dominant members. These techniques will work in many situations but may not be effective with bullies. It is possible that the group leader will have to talk to the bully privately during a break or after the meeting to ask him or her to respect the opinions of the others in the group. If this direct intervention doesn't work, the leader should consider asking the person who made the appointments to the committee to talk to the bully about his or her disruptive behavior.

Dealing with Peer Pressure

Most people are more comfortable if they feel they are a part of a group and not an outsider. Therefore, people have a tendency to go along with what they think the group believes or values, even if they don't necessarily agree. This can lead to "group think" in which the members place a higher value on agreement than on identifying multiple options. This problem is easiest to deal with at the very beginning of the process by making it clear that the group's task is to identify multiple options. The leader should assure the group that the purpose is not to make the final decision and that success will be defined by the number and creativity of the options identified. This, in turn, creates a group norm that supports and encourages diverse points of view.

Involving the Right People

Several things should be considered when determining whom to involve in the identification of options. First, of course, you want to include people who have something to contribute to the discussion. Their contributions may be based on specialized skills or expertise, on background or experience, or on position or authority. Second, you want to include people who care about the issue being considered. Third, you want to include people who will be affected by whatever option is ultimately selected. Finally, you want people who are reasonably open to change and willing to consider a variety of points of view. If you are careful in your selections (and lucky), most of the participants in whatever process you use to identify options could be included in at least three of these four categories.

Evaluating Methods of Identifying Options

Four methods you might use to help a group identify options are general group discussion, brainstorming, Nominal Group Technique, and the Delphi Method. Each of these methods can be used effectively in certain situations. The important thing is to match the method and the situation. Four measures that can be used to help you decide which method will be most effective for a given situation include the desired

> level of participation from the group
>
> range of the options identified
>
> skill required of the facilitator/leader
>
> time it takes to make the decision

Level of Participation

The first measure to use when deciding which method to use for identifying options is how much participation you need to identify the options for a specific decision. If the options you are to consider relate to a significant change in policy, you will probably want to use a process that encourages the maximum level of participation. On the other hand, if you are developing options for dealing with a situation in a single unit or dealing with a relatively minor change, you may not want or need extensive participation.

Range of Options Identified

The second measure is the range and creativity of the options that are identified. Some problems are intrinsically more difficult to address than others. Consider two committees, one responsible for identifying options for ways to integrate a new technology into the ongoing operations of the library and the second responsible for options for improving the activities for the annual staff day training event. Both are important, but the first will require considerably more flexibility and creativity than the second.

Leadership Skill Required

The third measure is the skill required to develop and lead the process to be used to identify the options. Some of the methods described in this appendix are relatively easy to manage; others require more specialized skills or knowledge.

Time Required

The final measure is the length of time it will take to identify options. The identification of options is just the first step in the decision-making process. There is not much point in expending so much effort on this part of the process that there is no time left to reach agreement on the most effective option to select before the deadline for implementation. Furthermore, some decisions are fairly simple or can only be addressed in a limited number of ways. As a general rule, select the easiest and quickest process that will produce the level of participation and range of options you need.

Methods for Identifying Options

General Group Discussions

Level of participation:
    Varies, often low
Range of options identified:
    Low to moderate
Leadership skill required:
    Low
Time required:
    Low

General group discussion is probably the most common method used for identifying options in libraries. Group discussions often occur during meetings that have multiple agenda items. Someone will raise an issue, someone else will suggest a solution, there may or may not be a little discussion, and the suggestion is adopted. The other common setting for group discussion is a special committee meeting called to review a problem and to identify possible solutions.

General group discussions present a number of problems when used as the means to identify options. Because general group discussions often occur extemporaneously, people don't have time to think about the problem and bring suggestions to the meeting. Instead, they are expected to think of options very quickly. The negative effects of peer pressure and the dominance of one or more members of the group are most likely to occur in this situation. Furthermore, the process of identifying options tends to end the first time someone suggests a solution that sounds reasonable to the other members of the group. There is no reward for prolonging the identification process, and there is often considerable pressure to move on to the next item on the agenda.

WHEN TO USE

Generally, library managers overuse group discussion. However, group discussion can be an effective way to identify options in several circumstances. The first is when the decision to be made is confidential and the number of people involved in the process of identifying options is small. Two or three people would probably find it difficult and obtrusive to use any of the other methods to identify options. It is also appropriate to use general group discussions to identify options when the group is one that meets regularly and has a shared knowledge base. Branch managers, for instance, often identify options for addressing common problems during their monthly meetings. However, in both instances, the people responsible for leading the process need to be very aware of the problems presented in the preceding paragraph and work with the members of the group to avoid them.

WHAT TO DO

1. Identify the issue or question to be addressed.
2. Select the group to address the question. It may be an existing group or committee, or it may be a group convened specifically for this process.
3. Prepare a brief (one-page) description of the issue to be addressed and send it to the members of the group at least one week prior to the meeting in which it will be discussed. Ask the participants to come to the meeting ready to suggest ways to address the issue.
4. At the meeting, briefly review the issue and ask the members to suggest options. Write the options on newsprint as they are presented. Encourage the group to provide as many suggestions as possible. Ask participants to clarify any options that seem

ambiguous. Encourage people to combine options that are similar. Do not evaluate the suggestions as they are proposed.

5. When it becomes clear that everyone is finished presenting options, review the list and ask if there are questions or additions. Make needed changes and develop a final list of options.

6. Use the options as the starting point for making a decision about the issue under review.

Brainstorming

Level of participation:
  Moderate to high
Range of options identified:
  Moderate
Skill of facilitator/leader:
  Moderate
Time required:
  Low to moderate

Brainstorming is a method used to identify multiple options by generating a large number of ideas through interaction among team members. The intent is to break free of preconceived ideas by exploring as many alternatives as possible and building on each other's ideas.

As shown in figure 36, in this process a group of people creates a list of ideas by having each member make a suggestion in turn, and the suggestions are recorded with no comment or discussion. Members are encouraged to build on each other's ideas. The actual brainstorming is best done in groups with six to eight members, but large groups can be divided into smaller groups for the initial brainstorming activity and then the suggestions from all of the small groups can be combined.

This is a relatively easy process to manage and, by its very nature, makes it difficult for a few people to dominate the discussion. It is a process that many people enjoy; participants often find the fast-paced generation of ideas by a variety of people stimulating. However, the fast pace of the process can be a problem too. Brainstorming doesn't provide much opportunity for reflection. Participants are encouraged to think of options very quickly, which may mean that more-complex or unusual options are never identified. Participants may also hesitate to make an unusual or creative suggestion for fear that others will laugh at them or think they are strange. There may be a tendency to follow the lead of the first two or three people who offer options rather than suggesting alternates that may be perceived as being in conflict with earlier recommendations.

FIGURE 36
Rules for Brainstorming

Rules for Brainstorming

1. Be creative; push the limits.
2. Never criticize anyone's ideas. There are no right answers or wrong answers.
3. The more ideas you contribute the better. Quantity is more important than quality.
4. Free-associate ideas; build on the ideas of others.
5. Don't discuss ideas or stop for explanations.
6. Record all ideas exactly as they are stated.
7. Take turns making suggestions. Contribute one idea each time it is your turn.
8. Pass your turn if you have no further suggestions.

WHEN TO USE

Brainstorming is a good method to use to generate a lot of ideas from a group in a fairly short period of time. It works best when it is used to consider a single, focused topic. For example, brainstorming can be an excellent way to identify a list of possible activities to achieve a predetermined goal and objective. However, it is probably not the best way to identify the options for addressing the myriad of issues surrounding access to pornographic sites on the Internet. In the first case, the staff of the library probably have all of the information they need to make suggestions, and any grouping of several dozen activities could be used to accomplish the goal and objectives. In the second case, there aren't dozens of good answers. In fact, there aren't any answers that satisfy everyone involved. Having people with little knowledge of the legal issues or the political environment make suggestions is probably not going to be useful.

WHAT TO DO

1. Identify the issue or question to be addressed.
2. Decide whom to include in the process. This may be an existing group or committee or it may be a group convened specifically for this process.
3. Decide if you want to have official recorders for each group or if you want to ask the participants to share the responsibility for recording.
4. Write a short issue statement. This should be specific enough to help participants focus on the issue but open-ended enough to encourage creativity. The statement could include a list of questions that would encourage exploration of the topic.
5. At the beginning of the brainstorming session, review the problem statement with the participants.
6. Prepare a handout with the rules for brainstorming (see figure 36), and distribute it to all participants.
7. If the group has more than eight people, divide it into smaller groups.
8. Establish a specific period of time for the initial brainstorming activity, usually around twenty minutes.
9. If there is more than one group working on the problem, combine their suggestions into a master list on newsprint.
10. Review and discuss the items on the master list, clarifying when necessary and combining when possible.
11. Use the options on the master list as the starting point for making a decision about the issue under review.

Nominal Group Technique

The Nominal Group Technique is used to generate a large number of ideas through contributions of members working individually. Research suggests that more ideas are generated by individuals working alone but in a group environment than by individuals engaged in group discussions.[2] In this process, group members start by writing down their ideas on note cards and posting them for others to read. Members get an opportunity to ask questions to clarify ideas and then they participate in group discussions about all of the ideas presented. Finally, each group member reassesses the ideas presented and selects those that seem most effective. These conclusions are then posted for a final discussion.

The Nominal Group Technique is both more time-consuming and more structured than brainstorming. The investment in time is often repaid because this process generally produces a greater number of more developed and creative ideas than are produced in a group discussion or brainstorming process. However, people generally feel more comfortable with the fast-paced and open brainstorming process than with the Nominal Group Technique, at least partly because people are more familiar with brainstorming. The Nominal Group Technique structure can be perceived by group members as being artificial and restrictive. Participants may feel that the process drives the content, rather than the other way around, and as a result, they may question the validity of the final list of options.

WHEN TO USE

The Nominal Group Technique is a good method to use with a group that has some very strong or opinionated members. Because each participant writes down his or her ideas privately before any discussion begins, the responses are less likely to be driven by the dominant members of the group. Because the facilitator reads the suggestions aloud, the process allows suggestions to be evaluated on their own merits rather than being prejudged based on who made them. The Nominal Group Technique also can be used effectively to identify options for addressing issues that are potentially controversial. For instance, you may be considering how to revise your circulation policies so they support your goal of meeting the public's demand for materials on current topics and titles. This opens up some interesting possibilities, including extending your loan period, allowing patron reserves, etc. Each of these possibilities has proponents and opponents. Using this process, you can develop a comprehensive list of options without a lot of arguments. You can also get a sense of which options are perceived as having the potential for being the most effective.

WHAT TO DO

1. Identify the issue or question to be addressed.
2. Decide whom to include in the process. This may be an existing group or committee or it may be a group convened specifically for this process.
3. Write a short problem statement. This should be specific enough to help participants focus on the issue but open-ended enough to encourage creativity. The statement could include a list of questions that would encourage exploration of the topic.
4. At the beginning of the session, describe the process to be used and review the problem statement with the participants.
5. Give the participants five to ten minutes to write down their ideas on note cards without any discussion with others. Ask participants to use a new card for each idea.
6. Collect the cards and read the ideas, one at a time. Write the ideas on newsprint as they are read, so that everyone can see them. There is no discussion during this part of the process.

7. After all of the ideas have been recorded, encourage participants to discuss them. Participants may be asked to clarify their suggestions. They can express agreement or disagreement with any suggestion.

8. Give participants several minutes to select the five options they think are the most effective.

9. Tabulate choices and indicate which options received the most votes. One quick way to tabulate the choices is to use the dot exercise, described in Groups Reaching Agreement (Appendix C).

10. Discuss the final list of options.

11. Use the options as the starting point for making a decision about the issue under review.

Delphi Method

Level of participation:
  High
Range of options identified:
  Moderate to high
Skill of facilitator/leader:
  High
Time required:
  High

The Delphi Method was developed by the RAND Corporation as a way of eliminating the problems of generating ideas in groups: dominant behaviors, peer pressure, etc. In this process the participants never meet face-to-face, and they normally don't even know who the other members of the group are. The participants are presented with a list of general questions about a specific topic and asked to prepare a written response. The responses are sent to a coordinator who edits and summarizes them into a single report. This report is returned to the participants with a second list of questions intended to clarify differences, and participants are again asked to respond. The responses from the second round are edited and summarized and sent to the participants one final time. In this third round, participants are provided with statistical feedback about how the group responded to particular questions as well as a summary of the group's comments. This makes the participants aware of the range of opinions and the reasons for those opinions. The group is then asked to rank the responses one final time. A final report is developed and sent to all participants.

This is by far the most complex of the methods for identifying options, and most library staff members have never participated in a process that used the Delphi Method. The drawbacks are obvious. The method is quite time-consuming for the participants and extremely time-consuming for the coordinator. Furthermore, this method, more than any of the others, can be seriously compromised if the wrong people are included as participants because their involvement is so much more intensive. However, real benefits can be gained from using the Delphi Method as well. It can be used to gather options from people with significant subject expertise regardless of where they live. It can also be used to facilitate communication among individuals who disagree strongly about the issue being discussed.

WHEN TO USE

The Delphi Method is a process that library managers should use sparingly. It is simply too complex and too expensive to be used as a regular tool. However, in some circumstances the effort might well be worth the time and energy invested. For instance, let's say you are the director of a library in a community with a growing Latino population. You want to provide services for this new population group, but you don't know where to start. Some board and staff members feel that you don't have the resources to provide quality services to your "regular" client groups and that it would be foolish to reach out to new groups. In this instance, using the Delphi Method to generate options from board members, staff members, members of the Latino community, and librarians in other communities with established service programs for Latinos might be quite effective. It would minimize the potential for open conflict and maximize the number of options that could be considered. All points of view would be presented, and everyone involved would have a chance to respond. Because the responses are anonymous, participants may be more responsive to other points of view and more open to revising their initial suggestions.

WHAT TO DO

1. Identify the issue or question to be addressed.

2. Select a coordinator to manage the Delphi Method, preferably one who has coordinated a similar process before or at least participated in such a process.

3. Select the people to be involved in the process. The majority of Delphi studies have used between fifteen and twenty respondents.[3]

4. Send the participants a description of the process; include the time frame. Participants have to agree to respond to three sets of questions.

5. Prepare a brief description of the issue or problem to be addressed and develop a short list of questions to be answered. Send both to each of the members. The initial questions will probably be general and open-ended.

6. Edit the responses and develop a set of follow-up questions based on the answers to the first questions. These follow-up questions will be more specific than the first open-ended questions. Send the edited responses and the second questions to the participants.

7. Tabulate the responses to each question, edit the comments, and prepare a third report. Send this to the participants for review, and ask them to answer the questions one final time.

8. Tabulate the responses into a final report. Send copies to all participants. Use the information in the report as the starting point for making a decision about the issue under review.

NOTES

1. United Way, *Measuring Program Outcomes* (Alexandria, Va.: United Way of America, 1996).
2. Center for Rural Studies, *Guidelines for Using the Nominal Group Technique.* Available at http://crs.uvm .edu/ gopher/nerl/group/a/meet/Exercise7/b.html.
3. Barbara Ludwig, "Predicting the Future: Have You Considered Using the Delphi Methodology?" *Journal of Extension* (October 1997). Available at http://www.joe.org/joe/1997october/tt2.html.

Appendix E

Instructions and Workforms

Purpose of Workform 1

Use this workform to clarify what the audiences who will review, approve, or use the library's technology plan need to know.

Who Should Complete Workform 1

The person who initiates the planning process, usually the library director, should complete this workform.

Factors to Consider When Completing Workform 1

Limit your list of audiences to those who will review, approve, or use the plan. The objective of this exercise is to identify potential problems or roadblocks to adopting the plan once it is completed and to preempt those issues through planning. You will still be able to use the plan with other groups for information purposes, for example, as a marketing piece for the general public to let them know how the technology plan will improve services.

To Complete Workform 1

1. Enter in column A a name for each group audience you identify as having a review, approval, or use interest in the library's technology plan.

2. Enter P in column B if you believe that one or more members of this group should participate in the planning process. Enter I if you believe that providing information about the process will be sufficient to meet this group's information needs.

3. Enter in column C the pieces of information each group will want or need to see in the plan.

4. Under Planning Results, write a brief statement of your expectations of the process and summarize the data elements the resulting plan must contain. This is your charge to the technology planning committee.

5. Write your name and the date on the bottom of the form.

Factors to Consider When Reviewing the Form

1. Have you included all the audiences who could affect your ability to implement the plan?

2. Are your own intended results for the plan clearly stated in the Planning Results section?

3. Review this form with the committee chair and with the committee at its first meeting to be sure that the committee understands the plan results you expect.

List each of the audiences who will review, approve, or use the library's technology plan, e.g., board members, staff, other city or county departments. For each audience you identify, decide if there should be a representative from this audience participating in the planning process, or if this group simply needs to be kept informed as the plan develops. For each identified audience, list what key pieces of information will be important.

A. Audience	B. Inform (I) or Participate (P)	C. Need to Know

Once you have identified the information needs of your intended audience, develop a statement of the results you intend to achieve. This will be the charge you give to those you ask to develop the library's technology plan.

PLANNING RESULTS

_____

_____

_____

- _____

- _____

- _____

- _____

- _____

Prepared by: _____   Date: _____

Purpose of Workform 2

Use this workform to develop an inventory of the technology-supported services in your library.

Who Should Complete Workform 2

Members of the planning committee and technology support staff will complete the form for each unit (branch or department) in the library.

Factors to Consider When Completing Workform 2

1. Include all of the equipment you find in each unit, even if it is not actively in use at the moment. Unused equipment may be redeployable for other purposes.
2. Ask how each piece of equipment is actually used. Don't assume that equipment, especially staff equipment, is used as it is supposed to be.
3. In units with a large number of PC workstations or other equipment used in services, you may want to complete separate forms for each department in the facility. This will be especially true if you provide services to adults and children or teens in separate areas of the library and discourage each from using the other's areas. Completing separate forms will allow you to understand the relative distribution of technology among the populations served.
4. Committee members might wish to discuss and agree upon the short one- to three-word descriptions of services that will be used in column D of Parts 2 and 3. Agreeing on the vocabulary before you begin to gather the data will ease the compilation of data in Workform 3 later.

To Complete Workform 2

1. Enter the unit you are inventorying.

PART 1: Servers

2. Enter in column A a name for each server located in this branch or department. Use a descriptive name that indicates the function of the server, e.g., web server, print server, integrated library system (ILS) server.
3. In column B enter PS if the server primarily supports direct or indirect public service, or AF if the server primarily supports administrative functions. Administrative functions are defined as business applications that are not directly or indirectly related to the provision of library services. Make your choice on the basis of the primary purpose of the equipment. An e-mail server, for example, would be AF, even if you receive and respond to e-mail from the public because its primary purpose is to support staff communication. The ILS server, which supports circulation and cataloging as well as the OPAC, would be PS because it supports both direct and indirect public service.
4. Enter in column C short, one- to three-word descriptions of the service(s) supported by the equipment. You may have multiple services supported by a single server. For example, you may have both web server software and

customer authentication software running on a single piece of equipment.

PART 2: PC Workstations

5. Enter in column A a descriptive name for each PC or collection of PCs in this location. If the location has a group of PCs that all offer the same services (e.g., public Internet PCs), you can enter one name and use column B to enter the number of devices that match the description.
6. In column C enter PS if the workstation(s) primarily supports direct or indirect public service, or AF if the workstation primarily supports administrative functions. Workstations used by staff to provide direct public service, such as workstations on reference desks, will be PS. Workstations in staff areas, if they are primarily used by staff to do off-desk public service work (answering e-mail reference, selecting materials, developing documents for public use), will be PS. Workstations used for administrative purposes (internal word processing, payroll, budget, human resources management, etc.) will be identified by an AF. If a workstation is used for both public services and administrative services, identify it as a PS machine. Enter "None" in this column for equipment no longer in use.
7. Enter in column D short, one- to three-word descriptions of the service(s) supported by the equipment. You may have multiple services supported by a single workstation. For example, you may have both general Internet access and office automation applications running on a single piece of equipment. Enter "None" in this column for equipment no longer in use.

PART 3: Other Equipment Used in Services

8. Enter in column A a descriptive name for each piece of equipment or collection of equipment in this location. If the location has a group of equipment that all offer the same services (e.g., self-check machines), you can enter one name and use column B to enter the number of devices that match the description.
9. In column C enter PS if the equipment primarily supports direct or indirect public service, or AF if the equipment primarily supports administrative functions. Equipment used by staff to provide direct public service, such as digital scanners on reference desks or in staff work areas, even if they are sometimes used by staff to do administrative work (transmitting completed forms to headquarters), will be PS. Equipment used for administrative purposes, e.g., networked printers in administrative offices, would be AF. Enter "None" in this column for equipment no longer in use.
10. Enter in column D a short, one- to three-word description of the service supported by the equipment. Enter "None" in this column for equipment no longer in use.
11. Write your name and the date on the bottom of the form.

Factors to Consider When Reviewing the Form

Have you included all the locations and departments in your library, including administrative areas?

Location: _____

PART 1: Servers

A. Equipment	B. No.	C. PS or AF	D. Services Delivered

Prepared by: _____   Date: _____

Location: _____

PART 2: PC Workstations

A. Equipment	B. No.	C. PS or AF	D. Services Delivered

Prepared by: _____   Date: _____

Location: _____

PART 3: Other Equipment Used in Services

A. Equipment	B. No.	C. PS or AF	D. Services Delivered

Prepared by: _____   Date: _____

Strategic Plan Links: Sustain, Expand, or Phase Out

Purpose of Workform 3

Use this workform to summarize the information on technology-supported services gathered on Workform 2 and link it to the library's strategic service plan. This workform will also be used to record the committee's recommendations about whether services should be sustained, expanded, or phased out.

Who Should Complete Workform 3

The committee chair or a member of the committee can be appointed to complete column A prior to the committee discussion. A committee-appointed recorder should complete columns B and C during a meeting of the committee at which the links to the strategic plan and decisions about sustaining, expanding, or phasing out the services are discussed.

Factors to Consider When Completing Workform 3

It is possible that a single service will be linked to more than one strategic objective. It is also possible that a single strategic objective can be linked to more than one technology-supported service.

To Complete Workform 3

1. Enter in column A the descriptive name for each identified technology-based service currently offered by the library.

2. In column B identify the specific strategic plan objective that this service supports. If you can't find a direct link to the service plan, ask yourself if the service in question is a staff support or basic business function. If so, then enter "Admin/Staff" in column B.

3. In column C record the group's decision as to whether the service should be sustained, expanded, or phased out.

4. Use section D, Notes, to record any significant information that will inform others of why the committee made the decisions it did. As an alternative to completing this section, minutes from the meeting can be attached to the form if they contain the rationale for the decisions made.

5. Write your name and the date on the bottom of the form.

Factors to Consider When Reviewing the Form

1. Have you included enough information about why you made the decisions you did to inform other readers of the form?

2. Have you included on Workform 3 all of the services listed on the Workform 2s?

Strategic Plan Links: Sustain, Expand, or Phase Out

A. Service	B. Strategic Plan Links or Admin/Staff	C. Sustain (S) Expand (E) Phase Out (P)

Prepared by: _____   Date: _____

127

D.
Notes

_____
_____
_____
_____
_____
_____
_____
_____
_____
_____
_____
_____
_____
_____
_____
_____
_____
_____
_____
_____
_____
_____
_____
_____
_____
_____
_____
_____
_____
_____

Prepared by: _____   Date: _____

Purpose of Workform 4

Use this workform to summarize the information on technology-supported administrative services gathered on Workform 2. This workform will also be used to record the planning committee's recommendations about whether the services should be sustained, expanded, or phased out.

You will also use a copy of this workform, labeling it "New Projects," during Step 4.3 when you identify projects that will enhance your library's administrative functions.

Who Should Complete Workform 4

The committee chair or a member of the committee can be appointed to complete column A prior to the committee discussion. A committee-appointed recorder should complete column B during a meeting of the committee at which decisions about sustaining, expanding, or phasing out the services are discussed.

Factors to Consider When Completing Workform 4

It is possible that a single piece or a set of equipment on Workform 2 will be linked to more than one administrative function.

To Complete Workform 4

1. Enter in column A the descriptive name for each identified technology-based administrative function currently used in the library.

2. In column B record the group's decision as to whether the function should be sustained, expanded, or phased out.

3. Use section C, Notes, to record any significant information that will inform others of why the committee made the decisions it did. As an alternative to completing this section, minutes from the meeting can be attached to the form if they contain the rationale for the decisions made.

4. Write your name and the date on the bottom of the form.

Factors to Consider When Reviewing the Form

1. Have you included enough information about why you made the decisions you did to inform other readers of the form?

2. Have you included all of the administrative functions listed on the Workform 2s?

Administrative Tools: Sustain, Expand, or Phase Out

A. Function	B. Sustain (S) Expand (E) Phase Out (P)

Prepared by: _____ Date: _____

C.
Notes

_____

_____

_____

_____

_____

_____

_____

_____

_____

_____

_____

_____

_____

_____

_____

_____

_____

_____

_____

_____

_____

_____

_____

_____

_____

_____

_____

_____

_____

_____

Prepared by: _____   Date: _____

Purpose of Workform 5

Use this workform to evaluate the new public service support projects the committee has identified for possible inclusion in the plan.

Who Should Complete Workform 5

This workform is meant to be completed during a meeting of the planning committee where possibilities for new projects are discussed. A committee-appointed recorder should complete columns A through E during a meeting of the committee at which suggestions are made, the relevant strategic plan objectives are identified, and the relation to audience, outcomes, and appeal are discussed.

To Complete Workform 5

1. Enter in column A the descriptive name for each project under discussion.

2. In column B identify the specific strategic plan objective that this project supports. If you can't find a direct link to the service plan, ask yourself if the project in question is an administrative function. If so, then record it on a clean copy of Workform 4, Administrative Tools, and label it "New Projects."

3. In column C record the group's decision as to whether the project has a high, moderate, or low relation to the target audience identified in the strategic plan.

4. In column D record the group's decision as to whether the project has a high, moderate, or low relation to the intended outcomes identified in the strategic plan.

5. In column E record the group's decision as to whether the project will have a high, moderate, or low appeal to the target audience identified in the strategic plan.

6. Write your name and the date on the bottom of the form.

Factors to Consider When Reviewing the Form

1. Staff often feel compelled to somehow force a relationship between a project and an intended outcome. If you have to describe a particular set of circumstances to get the outcome to relate to the project, you are probably working too hard to "make it fit." A good match is usually immediately obvious to most committee members.

2. The target audience you identify should be the target audience in the strategic plan objective, not a group whose influence you are counting on to affect the target group. For example, don't assume that if your project really serves teachers or parents that they will somehow transfer their use to an audience identified in the strategic plan as children. You are looking for a direct one-to-one relationship, not a one-step-removed relationship.

3. Don't feel you need to include the moderate projects in your plan. If nothing you have identified seems to be right on target, you can look for more options, or you can put forward a technology plan that focuses on sustaining your existing programs.

A. Proposed Project	B. Strategic Plan/Objective	C. Relation to Target Audience	D. Relation to Intended Results	E. Appeal

1 = High   **2** = Moderate   **3** = Low

Prepared by: _____   Date: _____

Evaluating Efficiency Projects: Staff Savings

Purpose of Workform 6

Use this workform to collect the data needed to evaluate the new efficiency projects the committee has identified for possible inclusion in the plan.

Who Should Complete Workform 6

For each project under consideration, a committee member should be appointed to gather the information and perform the calculations.

Factors to Consider When Completing the Workform

General estimates of time spent and number completed are good enough at this stage. If greater accuracy is needed at a later stage in the planning process, additional data can be gathered at that time.

The best place to get estimates of time spent is from the people who actually do the work. You will have to ask the people doing the work about their workflow to understand how the project might change their activities.

Remember that there may be staff in a variety of job classifications involved at different stages in any task. Be sure you gather information for each stage that will be affected by the project.

If multiple people in a single job classification do the work under consideration, talk with several of them to develop an averaged estimate of time to be saved. It is not necessary to record each staff member's estimate separately.

To Complete Workform 6

1. Enter the name of the project on the top line.

2. For each job classification of staff involved in the task, collect the data in rows A and B. You will complete separate sets of information for each job classification. Enter the job classification title on the first line of each block of data.

3. In row A, enter the amount of time you anticipate will be saved by staff in this job classification if this project is implemented.

4. In row B, record the number of times per year the transaction is done by staff in this classification.

5. Multiply row A by row B. If row A is recorded in minutes, enter your answer in row C. If row A is recorded in hours, enter your answer in row D.

6. If you have entered data in row C, divide your answer by 60 to convert minutes to hours and record the result in row D.

7. Determine the average hourly cost for staff in this job classification and enter it in row E.

8. Multiply row D by row E and record your answer in row F.

Summary

9. Add together all of the completed row Ds and enter the result in row G.

10. Add together all of the completed row Fs and enter the result in row H.

11. Write your name and the date on the bottom of the form.

Factors to Consider When Reviewing the Form

1. Did you include all of the classifications of staff whose work will be affected by this project?

2. If the tasks affected by this project are not ones the library collects statistics on, you may have to dig a bit to develop an estimate of how many times a transaction occurs each year. It is usually easier to ask people to estimate per day or per week numbers and then multiply those numbers to get annual figures. If the person you are talking to can't begin to guess, help them by successively narrowing the choices, i.e., "Is it 1 or 100 times a week? Is it 5 or 50? Is it 10 or 30?" Most people can give reasonable approximations if you give them suggestions to react to.

Project: _____

Job classification: _____

A. Anticipated savings in time per transaction _____

B. Number of times each transaction is completed annually _____

C. Total anticipated time saved (minutes) _____

D. Total anticipated time saved (hours) _____

E. Average personnel cost per hour _____

F. Anticipated annual personnel cost savings _____

Job classification: _____

A. Anticipated savings in time per transaction _____

B. Number of times each transaction is completed annually _____

C. Total anticipated time saved (minutes) _____

D. Total anticipated time saved (hours) _____

E. Average personnel cost per hour _____

F. Anticipated annual personnel cost savings _____

Job classification: _____

A. Anticipated savings in time per transaction _____

B. Number of times each transaction is completed annually _____

C. Total anticipated time saved (minutes) _____

D. Total anticipated time saved (hours) _____

E. Average personnel cost per hour _____

F. Anticipated annual personnel cost savings _____

SUMMARY

G. Total anticipated time saved (hours) _____

H. Total anticipated annual personnel cost savings _____

Prepared by: _____   Date: _____

Purpose of Workform 7

This workform provides a format for recording the baseline of the library's technology and the possible upgrade and enhancement requirements of that technology.

Who Should Complete Workform 7

The library's technology support staff or members of the planning committee should complete this workform.

Factors to Consider When Completing Workform 7

You will be completing this form in stages as your planning process progresses.

To Complete Workform 7

1. Enter on line 1 a description of the group of technology covered in this form. Possible groups might include:
   * staff workstations and peripherals
   * public workstations and peripherals
   * servers
   * network equipment and circuits/bandwidth
   * server software
   * staff software applications
   * public software applications, with separate groups for children and adults if you have separate sets of software for each

2. Under Baseline Technology list all of the currently installed technology in the group covered by this form. Note the number of devices of each type in brackets after the description.

3. Under Retirement Targets list those items of currently installed technology that support services that the planning process will recommend phasing out.

4. Under Support Only list those items that can continue to function without upgrades for the foreseeable future.

5. Under Existing Commitments and Needed Upgrades, list any additions or upgrades that the library has already committed to make to this group of technology. Append the term "committed" to the entry to indicate that these are preexisting commitments, not projects from the current planning process.

    Also, list any upgrades that will be needed in this group within the next 12–18 months to sustain existing levels of service.

6. Under Developments to Monitor, note any future changes you have identified that might affect this group of technology, e.g., an expected release of the operating system or application software, or a new type of application or hardware you want to consider.

7. Under Issues and Dependencies enter any possible problems or warnings that may be associated with items in boxes 3, 5, or 8.

8. Under Future Possibilities three types of plans 2–3 years in the future may be recorded:
   * needed upgrades that will take place
   * existing infrastructure elements to be expanded
   * new infrastructure elements to be considered

    For upgrades that will be needed to sustain existing services in the next 2–3 years, append the term "sustain" to the entry.

    For existing services that are to be expanded, append the term "expand" to the entry.

    For new services to be considered, append the term "new" to the entry.

9. Write your name and the date at the bottom of the form.

Factors to Consider When Reviewing the Form

1. Have you identified all of the upgrades you know or suspect will be required? Ask your ILS vendor if any of the equipment it is maintaining will no longer be covered by maintenance agreements during the next 2–3 years.

2. Equipment under warranty, especially heavily used public access equipment, should be considered for replacement as the warranty period ends.

3. Mission-critical software (without which you cannot operate) should be kept within 1–2 releases of the current release to ensure that support will be available if needed.

1. Technology: _____

CURRENT	WITHIN 12–18 MONTHS	2–3 YEARS
2. Baseline Technology	**5. Existing Commitments and Needed Upgrades**	**8. Future Possibilities**
3. Retirement Targets	**6. Developments to Monitor**	
4. Support Only	**7. Issues and Dependencies**	

Prepared by: _____   Date: _____

Purpose of Workform 8

Use this workform to gather information on the technical skill level of each member of the library's staff.

Who Should Complete Workform 8

All staff members should complete Part 1 of the workform. Technology support staff should also complete Part 2.

Factors to Consider When Completing Workform 8

Provide the form to all staff to get a complete picture of the library's current skill set. In some libraries it may be appropriate to provide this form to some volunteers as well, if they are involved in tasks utilizing the library's technology.

The purpose of this workform is to get every staff member's honest assessment of their skill level in each of the identified areas. Everyone who is asked to complete the form should be assured that they will not be penalized in any way for their answers. This information will be used to identify the training needs of the staff.

To Complete Workform 8

For each listed skill, staff are asked to mark one of five O's, ranging from No Skill to Proficient, which most nearly represents their assessment of their skills in each area.

Factors to Consider When Reviewing the Form

1. Which, if any, skills did your staff mark as no or little experience? Are there enough staff to warrant developing an in-house training program or sending staff to a class?

2. If you have only a few staff with no or little experience in a particular skill, do you have staff proficient in that skill who could act as peer trainers?

3. Staff skill levels change constantly as the result of training and experience. You will want to reassess skills regularly, at a minimum once a year.

4. This form surveys a very generic set of basic technical and support skills. You may want to customize the skills listed to reflect your own library's needs.

Technical Skills Assessment

Name: _____

Work Area: _____

Job Classification: _____ **Date:** _____

Instructions

This form should only take you 10–15 minutes to complete. Black out the O that most nearly represents your own assessment of your skill in each of the areas listed below. This is not a test. This is a guide to help us learn more about what additional training we may need to offer our staff.

PART 1: Basic Technology Skills

Software	No Skill		Some Ability		Proficient
Create, format, save, print, and open a document using word processing.	O	O	O	O	O
Send, receive, read, and respond to e-mail messages.	O	O	O	O	O
Attach files to e-mail and read files received as attachments.	O	O	O	O	O
Print, save, and delete e-mail messages.	O	O	O	O	O
Retrieve a deleted e-mail message.	O	O	O	O	O
Get to a website when you know the address.	O	O	O	O	O
Follow a link on a web page.	O	O	O	O	O
Identify links previously used.	O	O	O	O	O
Use browser functions of back, forward, stop, and reload.	O	O	O	O	O
Mark a website for easy return.	O	O	O	O	O

Computer Operations

	No Skill		Some Ability		Proficient
Turn on and log in to the computer.	O	O	O	O	O
Find, open, and close a program.	O	O	O	O	O
Find, open, and close a file from within a program.	O	O	O	O	O
Switch to another running program.	O	O	O	O	O
Switch to another window within a program.	O	O	O	O	O
Move and resize a window.	O	O	O	O	O
Scroll through a document.	O	O	O	O	O
Double-click, right-click, drag and drop with a mouse.	O	O	O	O	O
Choose a dialog box option.	O	O	O	O	O

Prepared by: _____   **Date:** _____

Computer Operations (*cont.*)	No Skill		Some Ability		Proficient
Create, rename, and delete files and folders.	O	O	O	O	O
Move and organize files.	O	O	O	O	O
Shut down the computer.	O	O	O	O	O

Hardware

Add paper, change ink cartridge, clear paper jam in printers.	O	O	O	O	O
Locate on/off switches on all equipment in your work location.	O	O	O	O	O
Identify data cables and power cords on all equipment in your work location.	O	O	O	O	O

PART 2: Technical Support Skills

Equipment

Identify all installed equipment, including the network connection for each device.	O	O	O	O	O
Know how to reboot all equipment.	O	O	O	O	O
Find and change configuration and network settings in Windows, Apple, or Unix/Linux OS.	O	O	O	O	O
Install and configure printers.	O	O	O	O	O
Install and configure other peripherals.	O	O	O	O	O
Know how and when to use system maintenance tools such as defrag and scandisk.	O	O	O	O	O

Network

Troubleshoot network problems to isolate a problem.	O	O	O	O	O
Add or remove a device from the network.	O	O	O	O	O
Understand basic computer and networking terminology to communicate effectively with vendors.	O	O	O	O	O

Software

Install and deinstall software on workstations and servers.	O	O	O	O	O
Configure desktop security on public access PCs.	O	O	O	O	O
Perform data backup and restore data from backup.	O	O	O	O	O

Prepared by: _____   Date: _____

Purpose of Workform 9

This workform provides a format for recording the estimated costs of investments needed to sustain the library's current technology-based services.

Who Should Complete Workform 9

The library's technology support staff or members of the planning committee should complete this workform.

Factors to Consider When Completing Workform 9

There is likely to be considerable time between when this form is completed and when the library purchases the equipment. If you solicit more than one cost quote, record the average price for each item, not the lowest price you are quoted. This will protect you from budgeting too little.

If your own staff will be installing the equipment or software, you will need to ask them approximately how long they think it will take. You will also need to determine the average hourly wage of the staff who will do the work in order to estimate installation costs.

To Complete Workform 9

1. Enter a description of the equipment, software, or bandwidth to be purchased on line 1.
2. Enter the number of items to be purchased on line 2.
3. Enter the cost per item on line 3.
4. Multiply line 2 by line 3 and enter the answer on line 4.

5. If you intend to buy a warranty for the equipment or software, enter the unit price of the warranty on line 5. If you will not buy a warranty, or if the warranty is included in the purchase price, leave this line blank.
6. If there is an annual maintenance fee for the item, enter it on line 6.
7. Multiply line 5 or line 6 by line 2 and enter the result on line 7.
8. If the vendor will be doing the installation, enter the cost to install each item on line 8. If not, leave line 8 blank.
9. Multiply line 8 by line 2 and enter the result on line 9.
10. If your staff will be doing the installation, enter the time they estimate it will take on line 10. If staff will not be involved in the installation, leave line 10 blank.
11. Multiply line 10 by line 2 and enter the result on line 11. Express the results in hours.
12. Enter the average hourly wage of the staff who will do the installation on line 12.
13. Multiply line 11 by line 12 and enter the result on line 13.
14. If your supplier quoted any additional costs (e.g., staging, testing), enter those costs on line 14.
15. Add lines 4, 7, 9, 13, and 14 and enter the result on line 15.
16. Write your name and the date at the bottom of the form.

Factors to Consider When Reviewing the Form

Add all of the completed Workform 9s together to arrive at the total cost to sustain services.

1. Equipment, software, or bandwidth to be purchased:

_____

EQUIPMENT/SOFTWARE		
2. Number of items to be purchased		
3. Cost per item		
4. Total cost of items to be purchased		
WARRANTY/MAINTENANCE		
5. Cost of warranty per item		
6. Annual maintenance cost per item		
7. Total cost of warranty or annual maintenance		
INSTALLATION BY VENDOR		
8. Cost of installation per item		
9. Total cost of vendor installation		
INSTALLATION BY STAFF		
10. Time to complete installation per item		
11. Total time needed (in hours)		
12. Average hourly wage		
13. Total cost of staff installation		
ADDITIONAL SERVICES		
14. Cost of additional services		
15. Total Cost		

Prepared by: _____   Date: _____

Requirements of New or Expanded Services

Purpose of Workform 10

This workform provides a format for recording the data gathered on products and services that can be used to expand current technology-based services or introduce new services.

Who Should Complete Workform 10

Each member of the library's technology support staff or planning committee should complete this workform as they investigate products and services.

Factors to Consider When Completing Workform 10

Complete a separate copy of the workform for each vendor you contact.

To Complete Workform 10

1. Enter the project name.
2. Enter the name of the vendor and the name of the specific product discussed.
3. Enter a description of the hardware, software, or network equipment to be purchased. Alternately, if you have received a written quote from the vendor, attach it to the workform.
4. Enter the vendor's response to your question on the bandwidth requirements of the product.
5. Record if the vendor will supply all needed hardware. If not, note what pieces must be acquired from third parties. If the vendor suggests third parties, note them here.

6. Ask the vendor if the library can buy hardware or some software components from another source. Which components? Is there any reason why the vendor cautions against this? If so, record it here.
7. List the technical skills needed to install and configure the product.
8. List installation services available from the vendor and their costs.
9. List the technical skills needed to operate and support the product.
10. Describe the vendor's support services and their costs.
11. Write your name and the date at the bottom of the form.

Factors to Consider When Reviewing the Form

1. If you have multiple completed Workform 10s for a single project (different vendors, different products, same results), you will need to select one to recommend. You can either do that at this point, based on the factors in this workform, or wait until after you have completed Workform 11 to assess the technical support staff's ability to implement the options.
2. If you have only one copy of Workform 10 for each project, you can add all of the completed Workform 10s together to arrive at the total cost for new or expanded services.

Requirements of New or Expanded Services

1. Project Name: _____

2. Vendor/Product: _____

---

3. List hardware, software, and network requirements. Include all purchase costs.

4. List bandwidth requirements, if any.

5. Does vendor supply all needed hardware? If not, what must we get from third parties?

6. If the library chooses to, can we purchase any of the hardware or software from another supplier? If so, which pieces?

Prepared by: _____   Date: _____

7. What technical skills are needed to install and configure the product?

8. Does the vendor provide installation services? What services and at what cost?

9. What technical skills are needed in production operation of the product?

10. What type of ongoing service and support does the vendor offer for the product? At what cost?

Prepared by: _____   Date: _____

Purpose of Workform 11

This workform compares the technical skills that proposed new or expanded projects require with the technical skills available on the library's staff.

Who Should Complete Workform 11

The library's technology support staff or members of the planning committee should complete this workform.

Factors to Consider When Completing Workform 11

The information on the skills required to support each project is gathered from the vendors who will supply the hardware and software. If you have more than one source for hardware and software and their estimate of the technical requirements vary, complete separate workforms for each supplier.

Information on the skills of the staff will come from the staff themselves.

The estimated number of hours available can be calculated by determining the number of productive hours available, then subtracting the number of hours needed to maintain and administer current systems.

To Complete Workform 11

1. Enter the project name.
2. Enter the name of the vendor supplying the information.

3. In the first column, under Required Skills, list each skill the potential supplier identified as necessary to implement the project.
4. In the second column, under Staff Member, list the name of the staff member who has that skill. If no staff member currently has the necessary skill, leave the box blank.
5. Write your name and the date at the bottom of the form.

Factors to Consider When Reviewing the Form

1. If you received differing estimates of the technical skills needed, do you understand why those differences exist? Is it because the underlying technologies are different? Is it because one vendor provides more or different support services than the other? If you can't identify a reason for the difference, do you think one of the vendors is underestimating the requirements?
2. Do you have a completed Workform 11 for each completed Workform 10?
3. There may be skills listed for which you have not been able to enter a staff member's name. This doesn't automatically mean you can't include this project in your plan, but it will increase the difficulty factor when you evaluate projects in a later step.

Project Name: _____

Vendor: _____

REQUIRED SKILLS	STAFF MEMBER

Prepared by: _____   **Date:** _____

Purpose of Workform 12

This workform provides a format for recording the estimated time that will be required to implement a project. This form records the actual working days needed to complete the project steps, not the total elapsed time from start to finish of the entire project.

Who Should Complete Workform 12

The library's technology support staff or members of the staff who will be responsible for each project should complete this workform.

The people completing the form may need to talk with technology support staff to get estimates of the Maintenance Phase times.

Factors to Consider When Completing Workform 12

Be sure to include projects that sustain current services, as well as expanded services and new services projects, in developing time estimates.

Use the following definitions for the five stages when completing the form:

Needs Assessment is the phase of the project in which the functional and technical requirements are defined.

Selection is the formal process of acquiring the product and services. Typical activities include issuing RFPs, functional demonstrations, and completing purchasing processes.

Implementation typically includes hardware and software installation, configuration, testing, and training.

Maintenance is the period of ongoing use and support. Activities include system administration, user support, software upgrades, and enhancement.

Retirement is the purposeful decommissioning of a product or service and its removal from the library.

To Complete Workform 12

1. Enter the project name.
2. For each phase, enter the steps you expect will be required to complete the phase.
3. For each step you have entered, estimate the time, in days, you believe will be needed to complete the step. You are only estimating actual working days, not the total elapsed time the step will take.
4. Add the total number of days required for each phase and enter it in the Total line associated with each phase in the Total Days for Each Phase column.
5. Add the entries in the Total Days for Each Phase column and enter the result in Total for Project.
6. Estimate the additional hours per year you anticipate will be required to support this project in the maintenance phase and enter it in the Maintenance Phase row.
7. Write your name and the date at the bottom of the form.

Factors to Consider When Reviewing the Form

1. Have you included all of the major steps in each phase? It is not necessary at this point to develop an entire project plan, but be sure to include the big steps in your estimates.
2. Have you completed a copy of Workform 12 for every completed Workform 10 still under consideration?

Project Name: _____

STEPS	DAYS REQUIRED FOR EACH STEP	TOTAL DAYS FOR EACH PHASE
Needs Assessment		
Total, Needs Assessment Phase		
Selection		
Total, Selection Phase		
Implementation		
Total, Implementation Phase		
Retirement		
Total, Retirement Phase		
Total for Project		

Maintenance Phase	

Prepared by: _____   **Date:** _____

Instructions

Purpose of Workform 13

This workform gives you a place to summarize key information about the projects you are considering.

Who Should Complete Workform 13

The members of the planning committee should complete this workform.

Factors to Consider When Completing Workform 13

You have all of the data needed for this form in other forms you have already completed. Use this form only if a quick summary of the other forms will help the committee with its review and decision making.

To Complete Workform 13

1. Use one row of the form for each project.

2. In column A enter the name of the project. The names of the projects you will be entering are those on the list the planning committee created at Step 4.4 in the planning process, when working with Workforms 3, 4, and 5.

3. Enter the service objective addressed by this project in column B. This information can be found on Workform 3. If the project addresses an administrative or staff need, enter "Admin/Staff" in this box.

4. Enter an S for a project that sustains current services, an E for a project that expands current services, or N for a new service in column C.

5. Enter the estimated cost of the project in column D. This information can be found on Workform 9 or 10.

6. Enter the estimated number of days or weeks of staff time it will take to implement this project in column E. Remember this is actual work time, not elapsed time. This information can be found on Workform 12. *Note:* All of the projects' durations should be converted to the same unit of staff time, either days or weeks, before being entered on Workform 13.

7. Enter the name of the staffer who has the necessary skills and is the likely project leader in column F. Enter N if the necessary skills are not currently available. This information can be found on Workform 11.

8. During a committee meeting to discuss the information on this workform, decisions will be made about whether the projects listed will be easy or challenging for the library staff to complete. Use column G to record the committee's decisions.

9. During the same meeting, the committee will decide whether the projects listed will be costly or inexpensive. Use column H to record the committee's decisions.

10. Use column I to record the priority the committee assigns to each project. Use a pencil because the priorities may change as your discussions continue.

11. Write your name and the date at the bottom of the form.

Factors to Consider When Reviewing the Form

1. Rather than use the written form, you might want to enter this data into an electronic spreadsheet or database. This will make it easier to sort the projects based on various criteria (e.g., by service objective, or in order of cost or implementation time) during Step 7, the selection process.

2. Deciding whether a project is easy or challenging and inexpensive or costly depends on the staff's skill level and the library's budget. There are no objective definitions of these terms; you must make these decisions based on your own environment.

Summary of Projects

A. Project Name	B. Service Objective or Admin/Staff	C. Sustain, Expand, or New	D. Estimated Cost	E. Days to Complete	F. Skills Available	G. Easy or Challenge	H. Costly or Inexpensive	I. Priority

Prepared by: _____

Date: _____

Purpose of Workform 14

This workform is used to record the assumptions about available technology or costs that lead the planning committee or the project manager to make decisions about specific technologies to use in the future.

Who Should Complete Workform 14

The project manager should complete this workform, in conjunction with the planning committee members as needed.

Factors to Consider When Completing Workform 14

This form will be needed only for those projects that will be implemented in multiyear stages or in the later years of a multiyear technology plan.

To Complete Workform 14

1. Enter the name of the project.
2. Enter the stage(s) or step(s) at which the trigger point assumptions should be reviewed before proceeding.
3. Enter the specific decision that needs to be revisited before proceeding.
4. In the sections numbered 1–4, enter the reasons why the specific recommended technology was chosen.
5. Write your name and the date at the bottom of the form.

Factors to Consider When Reviewing the Form

Are the reasons listed on the form still valid as this stage or step of the implementation is about to begin? If not, what additional investigation needs to be done before this implementation can proceed?

Project: _____

Stage/Step: _____

Trigger Point Decision: _____

_____

Assumptions:

1. _____

_____

_____

_____

_____

_____

2. _____

_____

_____

_____

_____

_____

3. _____

_____

_____

_____

_____

_____

4. _____

_____

_____

_____

_____

_____

Prepared by: _____   Date: _____

153

Purpose of Workform 15

This workform is used by staff to suggest technologies for the library to consider adding to the technology plan.

Who Should Complete Workform 15

Any staff member with a suggestion should be encouraged to complete the form and submit it to the Project Prioritization Committee.

Factors to Consider When Completing Workform 15

If you are making a service improvement suggestion, use the library's strategic plan to complete section D of the workform.

To Complete Workform 15

1. Enter your suggestion in section A.
2. Explain how you believe the project will benefit the library in section B.

3. Check which type of suggestion you are making, a cost savings suggestion or a service improvement suggestion, in section C.
4. If you checked "service improvement," identify which of the library's service objectives are supported in section D.
5. If you checked "service improvement," identify the target audience for your suggestion in section E.
6. If you checked "cost savings," identify which department in the library you think will achieve the cost savings.

Factors to Consider When Reviewing the Form

Are the benefits identified consistent with the library's service and efficiency objectives? Just because something might be faster or easier doesn't make it worth an investment if it doesn't further the organization's goals.

A. Suggestion: _____

_____

_____

B. How will the library benefit from this suggestion? _____

_____

_____

C. [Check one] This is a:

☐ service improvement suggestion → Go to Step D

☐ cost savings suggestion → Go to Step F

D. Which of the strategic plan service objectives will be supported by this suggestion? _____

_____

_____

E. Who is the target audience for this service? _____

_____

_____

F. Which department within the library will achieve the projected cost savings? _____

_____

_____

G. How did you discover this technology? Please attach any additional information you may have about it. _____

_____

_____

Prepared by: _____   Date: _____

155

Instructions

Purpose of Workform 16

Use this workform to develop an inventory of your current technical infrastructure if your library does not already have an inventory.

Who Should Complete Workform 16

The technology support staff should complete this form. If your entire library technology support staff is on the planning committee, other committee members may want to help complete the inventory.

Factors to Consider When Completing the Form

You should have an entry on Workform 16 for each piece of equipment installed in your library. Include equipment that you own but may not be using, unless you decide as a part of the inventory process to discard it.

Much of the needed information for workstations and servers can be found by querying the devices themselves.

To Complete Workform 16

1. Enter the name of the location where this inventory is conducted.

A. Desktop Hardware

2. Use one row per device to complete this inventory.

3. In column 1 enter the location of the device in the library, e.g., Elm Branch, Adult Services, computer lab.

4. In column 2 enter the name of the specific workstation, e.g., Circulation 1.

5. In column 3 enter the type and speed of the processor in the workstation, e.g., Pentium 133MHz.

6. In column 4 enter the total hard drive capacity of the workstation followed by the total unused capacity. Separate the two numbers with a slash.

7. In column 6 enter the operating system name and release number, e.g., Windows 2000, Windows XP.

8. In column 7 enter Y if the workstation is network connected and N if it is a stand-alone device.

B. Servers

9. Follow instructions 1 through 7 for the library's servers.

C. Peripherals

10. Use one row per device to complete this inventory.

11. In column 1 enter the location of the device in the library, e.g., Elm Branch, Adult Services, computer lab.

12. In column 2 enter the name of the specific device, e.g., circulation receipt printer 1. If the library's peripherals are not named, use a combination of the location, manufacturer, model number, and device type, e.g., circulation HP 4050 printer.

13. In column 3 enter Y if the device is network connected or shared through a networked workstation. Enter N if it is connected to a single workstation and is not shared.

D. Local Area Networks

14. Use one row per network to complete this inventory.

15. In column 1 enter the location of the network in the library, e.g., Elm Branch, Adult Services, computer lab.

16. In column 2 enter the bandwidth of the network.

17. In column 3 enter the number of devices attached to the network.

E. Wide Area Networks

18. Use one row per connection to complete this inventory.

19. In column 1 enter the starting location of the WAN connection, e.g., Elm Branch.

20. In column 2 indicate where data goes over this circuit, e.g., library computer room, Internet, City/County IT.

21. In column 3 enter a description of the type of circuit, e.g., phone company frame relay, phone company digital data service, cable TV, city fiber.

22. In column 4 enter the bandwidth of the circuit. If the circuit is asymmetric, enter the downstream bandwidth followed by the upstream bandwidth and separate the two numbers with a slash.

Location: _____

A. Desktop Hardware

1. Location	2. Device Name	3. Processor	4. RAM	5. Disk Total/Available	6. Operating System	7. Network

Prepared by: _____   Date: _____

B. Servers

1. Location	2. Device Name	3. Processor	4. RAM	5. Disk Total/Available	6. Operating System	7. Network

Prepared by: _____

Date: _____

C. Peripherals

1. Location	2. Name	3. Network

Prepared by: _____ Date: _____

D. Local Area Networks

1. Location	2. Bandwidth	3. Number of Devices Attached

E. Wide Area Networks

1. Location	2. Connected to	3. Connection Type	4. Bandwidth

Prepared by: _____   Date: _____

Index

Diane Mayo is vice president of Information Partners, Inc., a library management and technology consulting firm that specializes in assisting libraries with planning and implementing a wide range of technologies, identifying appropriate staffing levels, and developing needed competencies to use technology well in the delivery of services. A professional librarian with more than twenty years' experience in the field of library automation, she speaks frequently on managing technology and technology-enhanced services in public libraries.

In addition to her consulting work, Diane has managed both technical services and public services operations in multi-branch public libraries and has worked for a vendor of automated library systems. Her other books include two PLA management guides, *Managing for Results: Effective Resource Allocation in Public Libraries,* coauthored with Sandra Nelson and Ellen Altman, and, with Jeanne Goodrich, *Staffing for Results: A Guide to Working Smarter.*